AF572290

# Scarecrow Poetry

## The Muse in Post-Middle Age

Edited by

Robert McGovern and Stephen Haven

The Ashland Poetry Press
Ashland University
Ashland, Ohio 44805

Copyright © 1994 By The Ashland Poetry Press

All rights reserved. Except for brief quotations in critical reviews, this book, or parts thereof, must not be reproduced in any form without permission in writing from the publisher. For further information, contact The Ashland Poetry Press, Ashland University, Ashland, OH 44805

Printed in the United States of America

ISBN 0-912592-36-2

Library of Congress Catalog Card Number 94-71673

Cover: Scarecrow by Rene Becker, Austin Nichols, Steve Owens, and Jason Thomas. Photograph by Randy Sarvis.

The Ohio Arts Council helped fund this organization with state tax dollars to encourage economic growth, educational excellence and cultural enrichment for all Ohioans.

# Acknowledgments

## Grateful acknowledgment is made to the following publications for permission to publish the following poems:

"Anniversary," "Sensual Music," "Our Tree," and "New Year's Day," by Philip Appleman, appeared previously in ***Let There Be Light*** (HarperCollins, 1991). Copyright © 1991 by Philip Appleman. Reprinted by permission of HarperCollins.

"Over His Dead Body," by Russell Atkins, appeared previously in ***The Record***, Vol. 1, (1988) and was reprinted in the booklet, ***Juxtapositions*** 1991. © 1991 by Russell Atkins.

"Crucifixion," "A Backyard in California," "Pray You Young Woman," "Tanck's Song About His Unicameral Mind," and "Eolian," by Hayden Carruth, appeared previously in his ***Collected Shorter Poems*** (Copper Canyon Press, 1992). Reprinted by permission of the poet.

"My friend," by Jane Cooper, first appeared in ***Nimrod***, 1991. Reprinted by permission of the poet. "Childhood in Jacksonville, Florida," by Jane Cooper, first appeared in ***Aphra***, 1975. Reprinted by permission of the poet. "My friend" and "Childhood in Jacksonville, Florida," by Jane Cooper, are forthcoming in ***Green Notebook, Winter Road*** (Tilbury House, Publishers, 1994)."Blue Anchor," by Jane Cooper, first appeared in ***Pequod***, 1979, and appeared also in ***Scaffolding: Selected Poems*** (Tilbury House Publishers, 1993). Reprinted by permission of the poet.

"Age," "Oh," and "Funny," appeared previously in ***Windows*** (New Directions, 1990). Copyright © 1990 by Robert Creeley. Reprinted by permission of New Directions.

"Mai-tai Music," by Madeline DeFrees, appeared previously in ***Image*** (Seattle Arts Commission Annual, Vol. X, 1992). Reprinted by permission of the poet. "A Visitor's Guide to the Lewisburg Cemetery" and "Spiritual Exercises," by Madeline DeFrees, appeared previously in ***Possible Sibyls*** (Lynx House Press, Amherst, MA, 1991). Reprinted by permission of the poet.

"Confession," by John Dickson, first appeared in "Quartet" and previously in ***Benchmark*** (University of Illinois Press, 1988). Reprinted by permission of the poet.

"Three Trees," by Robert Funge, appeared previously in ***The Bridge*** (Vol. 1, No. 2, Spring/Summer 1991). Reprinted by permission of the poet. "The Old Man of San Carlos," by Robert Funge, appeared previously in ***The Lie the Lamb Knows*** (Spoon River Poetry Press, 1979). Reprinted by permission of the poet.

"Golden Age," by Mac Hammond, appeared previously in ***Epoch*** (Winter/Fall 1983) and also in ***Estatic Occasions/ Expedient Forms*** (Macmillan, 1987). Reprinted by permission of the poet.

"The Ash," by William Heyen, appeared previously in ***Lord Dragonfly: Five Sequences*** (New York: Vanguard Press, 1981). Reprinted by permission of the poet.

"Stop the Deathwish! Stop It! Stop!" and "Jogger," are from ***Hang-Gliding from Helicon***, by Daniel Hoffman. Copyright © 1986 by the author, published by Louisiana State University Press. Used with permission.

David Ignatow, "43," "46," and "59," from ***Shadowing the Ground***, Copyright © 1991 by David Ignatow (Wesleyan University Press, 1991) is reprinted by permission of University Press of New England.

"Listening to Dvorak's Serenade in E" and "Seven Stages of Skeletal Decay," by Colette Inez, appeared previously in ***Alive and Taking Names*** (Ohio University Press, 1978). Reprinted by permission of the poet.

"the virgin who remembers," by William Inman, appeared previously in *Star Route Journal* (1991). Reprinted by permission of the poet.

"The Chosen" and "Figure," by Josephine Jacobsen, appeared previously in *The Sisters* (1987). Reprinted by permission of the poet. "Finally," by Josephine Jacobsen, appeared previously in *The Chinese Insomniacs* (1982). Reprinted by permission of the poet.

"Yahrzeit" and "On a Photograph of Myself as Grandmother," by Shirley Kaufman, appeared previously in *River of Salt* (Copper Canyon Press, 1993). Copyright © 1993 by Copper Canyon Press. Reprinted by permission of Copper Canyon Press.

"Five & Dime, Late Thirties," by X.J. Kennedy, appeared previously in *Boulevard* (Fall 1993). Reprinted by permission of the poet. "Old Masquerade," by X.J. Kennedy, appeared previously in *The Epigrammatist* (April 1991). Reprinted by permission of the poet.

"Spring Training," by Maxine Kumin, appeared previously in *Witness* (December 1992). Reprinted by permission of the poet.

"Two Magnets" and "Evening Train," by Denise Levertov, appeared previously in *American Poetry Review* (Volume 19, No. 5, November/December 1990) and were collected in her book *Evening Train* (New Directions, 1992). Copyright © 1992 by Denise Levertov. Reprinted by permission of New Directions.

"My Father With Cigarette 12 Years Before the Nazis Could Break His Heart," by Philip Levine, appeared previously in *The Forward*, 1992. Of the other two poems by Philip Levine, "Soul" appeared previously in *Three Penny Review*, 1993, and "February 14th," in *The New Yorker*. All three poems are reprinted with permission of Philip Levine. Copyright © 1994 by Philip Levine.

"A Man of Experience," by Mordecai Marcus, appeared previously in *Return from the Present* (New Editions Press, 1977). Reprinted by permission of the poet.

"Last Words of Methuselah," by Neill Megaw, appeared previously in *Negative Capability* (Vol. XII-1/2, 1993). Reprinted by permission of the poet.

"Love Poem 1990" is reprinted from *Liquid Paper: New and Selected Poems*, by Peter Meinke. The poem appears here with the permission of the University of Pittsburgh Press. Copyright © 1991 by Peter Meinke.

"In Memory of Rita Hayworth," by Richard Moore, appeared previously in *Chronicles* (April 1990) and was collected in his book *No More Bottom* (Orchises Press, 1991). Copyright © 1991 by Richard Moore. "The Cinder," by Richard Moore, appeared previously in *Agni Review* (Volume 37, Spring 1993). "The Old Man," by Richard Moore, appeared previously in *The Lyric* (Volume 73, No. 2, Spring 1993). All three poems are reprinted with the permission of the poet.

"Midwinter Notes," by Lisel Mueller, appeared previously in *The Georgia Review* (Winter 1992). Reprinted by permission of the poet. "What Is Left to Say" and "Fugitive," by Lisel Mueller, appeared previously in *Second Language*: Copyright © 1986 by the author, published by Louisiana State University Press. Used with permission.

"The Old Poet," by Leonard Nathan, appeared previously in *Salmagundi* (No. 96, Fall 1992). Reprinted by permission of the publisher. "Truth," by Leonard Nathan, appeared previously in *Zyzzyva* (VIII: No. 3, Fall 1992). Reprinted by permission of the publisher. "Vision in the Ice Cream Parlor," by Leonard Nathan, appeared previously in *Witness* (VII: No. 1, 1993). Reprinted by permission of the publisher. "Retirement Home Canticle," by Leonard Nathan, appeared previously in *Art/Life* (Vol. 9, No. 3, 1989). Reprinted by permission of the publisher.

"Narcissus at 60," by Linda Pastan, appeared previously in *The New Republic* (Vol. 209, No.

10, Sept. 1993). Reprinted by permission of the poet. This and all other poems by Linda Pastan included in this anthology are forthcoming in *An Early Afterlife*, due from Norton in 1995. "May 27," by Linda Pastan, appeared previously in *American Scholar* (Spring 1993). Reprinted by permission of the poet. "Sometimes," by Linda Pastan, appeared previously in *The Atlantic Monthly* (Vol. 272, No. 2, August 1993). Reprinted by permission of the poet. "Hardwood," by Linda Pastan, appeared previously in *The Virginia Quarterly Review* (Vol. 69, No. 1, Winter 1993). Reprinted by permission of the poet.

"The Land: A Love Letter" and "Survivor's Song," by Robert Phillips, appeared previously in *Personal Accounts: New & Selected Poems, 1966-1986* (Ontario Review Press, 1986). Reprinted by permission of Ontario Review Press.

"A Special Occasion," by Knute Skinner, appeared previously in *The Bears and Other Poems* (Salmon Publishers, 1991). The poem is reprinted with the permission of the author.

"An Envoi, Post-Turp" and "Anniversary Verses," by W.D. Snodgrass, appeared previously in *The Southern Review* and are collected in Snodgrass's *Each in His Season* (BOA Editions, 1993). Reprinted by permission of BOA Editions.

"Bob Summers' Body," by Gerald Stern, appeared previously in *Leaving Another Kingdom: Selected Poems* (Harper and Row Publishers, 1990). Copyright © 1990 by Gerald Stern. Reprinted by permission of Gerald Stern and HarperCollins. "Odd Mercy" appears here with permission of the author. Copyright © 1994 by Gerald Stern.

"Thread" is reprinted by permission of The University of Alabama Press from *A Belfry of Knees*, by Alberta Turner. Copyright © 1983 by The University of Alabama Press.

"To a Dead Flame," and "Elderly Sex," by John Updike, appeared previously in his *Collected Poems, 1953-1993* (Alfred A. Knopf Inc., 1993) Reprinted by permission of the publisher.

"The Last Day and the First," by Theodore Weiss, appeared previously in *Poetry* and was collected in his book *The Last Day and the First* (Macmillan, 1968). Copyright © 1968 by Theodore Weiss. Reprinted by permission of the poet. "An Old Cart," by Theodore Weiss, appeared previously in *Poetry* and was collected in *A Sum of Destructions*. Copyright © 1994 by the author, published by Louisiana State University Press. Used with permission.

"Old Houses" and "Old Love," by Ruth Whitman, appeared previously in *Laughing Gas: New and Selected Poems* (Wayne State University Press, 1991). Reprinted by permission of the poet.

"Playing" and "How She Goes," by John Woods, appeared previously in *Black Marigolds* (University Presses of Florida, Gainsville, Florida, 1994). Reprinted by permission of the poet. "Tulip Trees," by John Woods, appeared previously in *Black Marigolds*. Reprinted by permission of the poet.

"Mastectomy," by Nancy Means Wright, appeared previously in *The Bridge*. Reprinted by permission of the publisher.

"Grace Enters Armageddon," by Nancy Means Wright, appeared previously in *The Carolina Quarterly* (Vol. 43, Spring 1991). Reprinted by permission of the poet.

The Ashland Poetry Press wishes to thank the following for their invaluable editorial assistance: Deborah Cochran, Kim Damiano, Colleen Dean, Nancy Grimm, Tasha Kalista, and Erin Sweet.

# Contents

# Scarecrow Poetry

Folklore and a few "creativity" theorists tell us that poetry is the province of the young. Indeed, the young Keats in "Ode to a Nightingale" is essentially concerned with "youth [growing] pale, and spectre-thin" and dying, as well as with the youthful concern for time, "Where Beauty cannot keep her lustrous eyes,/ Or new Love pine at them beyond to-morrow...." He gives short shrift, and perhaps less understanding, to the groaning "Where palsy shakes a few, sad, last gray hairs...." Almost always a positive thinker, Robert Browning, at fifty-two (a fairly ripe age in the second half of the nineteenth century), writes "Grow old along with me!/The best is yet to be," which contemporary poet William Sylvester parodies with "Oh shrivel along/ With me, the worst is yet to be."

I mean here to define a subject matter genre that is essentially twentieth-century, though it goes back at least as far as Sophocles, who wrote *Oedipus at Colonus* when he was 90. Edmund Waller, who lived 81 years of the seventeenth century, tells us in "Of the Last Verses in the Book,"

> The soul's dark cottage, battered and decayed,
> Lets in new light through chinks that time has made;
> Stronger by weakness, wiser, men become
> As they draw near to their eternal home.
> Leaving the old, both worlds at once they view,
> That stand upon the threshold of the new.

In our time the examples of Thomas Hardy, who was a young writer when "the best is yet to be" was written, and W.B. Yeats, one of the venerable fathers of modernism, have not been enough to trim the romantic notion that poets reach their apex early, allowing them, according to social psychologist D.K. Simonton, "to die at tragically early ages and still find a place in the annals of history."

For many reasons the genre must be seen to reach its

fullness in the latter half of this century, primarily because of our demographics. People, including poets, are living longer. When we began this century, the average life-span was 49 years, and by 1990, largely because of better diet and health care, we reached an average of 76 years; those who know about such things suggest we'll put on another nine years by the turn of the century. But with the exception of William Butler Yeats (if we consider Hardy essentially a Victorian), not too many of the first generation modernists wrote poetry dealing with advanced (or post) middle-age. Allen Tate, for example, has a large gap of years between his terza rima poems that were to be his magnum opus and three poems of good-by to his wife and children, which are his only poems that fit the genre. John Crowe Ransom spent his later years puttering with poems he had written much earlier in life, and, I've been given to understand, in his last years created many problems for editors with this puttering. Robert Penn Warren, however, continued to write and gave the world some very important scarecrow poetry--the term I have settled upon for defining the genre.

Scarecrow comes, of course, from Yeats. In my correspondence with various poets about the concept, I used the term "old fart," which most seemed delighted with and which has a tone that is necessary to an understanding of the genre. I suspect I am adopting Yeats as a convention for my argument because he lived so long and, indeed, was a part of the Decadents (those precious Victorian rebels in the 1890s) before embracing modernism. He wrote much and well about a "country for old men," "a comfortable kind of old scarecrow," and the "foul rag-and-bone shop of the heart." He wrote, moreover, until the end and demonstrated that while an "aged man is but a paltry thing," he could in his later years surpass in perception much of his early verse. Yeats did not give up writing after his youth, or even middle age, and I think that the examination of poetry of later years finds most poets who are not overcome by the romantic concept (or whatever else might cause the writing drive to flag) are bound to be at the height of their powers in the scarecrow time of life. It would seem that the generation or two of poets following the advent of modernism have most exploited the heart's "rag-and-bone shop."

If older poets are writing, for whom? Daniel Hoffman asked, "Has anyone remarked on the fact that almost the only audiences to whom poetry can be read aloud are aged between 18 and twenty-one years old? What effect might that have on the poems being written?" Part of the answer comes from my surgeon, whose specialty is clogged arteries and whose husband is a literary scholar: "Poetry is very necessary," she says simply. While my doctor answers in terms of the patient's emotional necessities, Hoffman answers his own question from the poet's viewpoint: "of course good poets deal with the truths of their feelings; as one approaches the condition of sans hair, sans eyes, sans teeth, sans everything, a different set of feelings displaces the optimism of youthfulness."

So, with the evolution of the world's demographics, the waning of the romantic folklore about youth and poetry, and the need for a poetic response to the "different set of feelings," scarecrow poetry seems to be coming to full flower and is partaking of the husbandry that began with Sophocles. It therefore behooves us to note the nature of what the many scarecrows in our time are doing in the field.

Certainly a predominant mark of the majority of poets who have lived beyond Byron's age is self-irony. Given the vitality of the poetry of this genre, calling it the poetry of old age is unacceptable, geriatric poetry is far too clinical, and the poetry of advanced-middle age is a terrible euphemism. (An academic colleague has suggested "geezer" poetry, which could serve, at best, as an occasional aside.) It has to be called something like old fart or scarecrow poetry--all us golden agers know that.

Well then, how do poets, who try to speak for their world, understand the scarecrow sensibility? Denise Levertov in a poem called "Evening Train" calls the problem into question as she describes someone she calls "An old man sleeping in the evening train" but remembers her own age and must "acknowledge he's likely/ no older than I. But in the dimension/ that moves with us but itself keeps still/ like the bubble in a carpenter's level, I'm fourteen." She asserts that "Everyone has an unchanging age (or sometimes two)/ carried with them, beyond expression," and speculates on the "unchanging age" that the old man carries with him as "The train moves through the dark quite swiftly.../with its load of people, each/ with a known age and that other,/ the hidden one...." She concludes her poem with an image not unlike the one of the bubble in the level.

Poets, of course, are always making something out of what they don't quite understand, coming to, perhaps, a tentative insight. Mordecai Marcus in "Refusing Codgerdom" sees a way of managing his situation as an aging professor by wrapping himself "in a codger's hide." He spread his jaws to a "heh! heh! heh!/...winked at shifty goings on" in the hall and the like. But when reaching "to stroke the carpet of [his] beard" and finding instead that his chin "was a bare sexy thrust," his self-vision is altered.

All good poems are individual, unique, but all, T.S. Eliot tells us, partake of a tradition and cannot really be new unless they do. The tradition of scarecrow poetry goes back as far as Sophocles, and other traditions that this genre depends on have always been with us: the shock of recognition; our knowledge of the stages of man; the joy of bodily functions; loneliness; sickness; endurance; death. These concerns certainly overlap and flow into one another, but for purposes of discussing this developing genre, I'm going to try to create some useful categories, and I'll try to put them in something of a reasonable sequence.

Certainly we should begin with poems on the realization of old age, and indeed it would seem that there is always something of a shock in that recognition, even, or especially, if our secret age be fourteen. Donald Hall recounted to me the following:

I remember John Ashbery telling me, years ago,

> when we were in our forties I suppose, "I thought I had managed to write a poetry that had absolutely no subject matter at all...and then I discovered that all my poems were about...*aging*." I don't mean to say that I really quote him word for word, but it was pretty much like that.
>
> And certainly the same is true of my own, except that I always thought I had subject matter--I just didn't realize that I had only one kind of subject matter.

Hall was writing poems about getting old when he was twenty-five, as in "My Son My Executioner," (*Old and New Poems*., Ticknor and Fields, N.Y., 1990, p. 19) where the child's "cries and hungers document/ Our bodily decay." And it is perhaps true that while there is always shock in the revelation, it isn't necessarily sudden. In his "The Day I Was Older," (IBID. p. 186) written much later, Hall names objects and instances that have marked his epiphanies: "The Clock" defines passage as being upon the sea; in "The News" he reads obits and finds that an old friend, Emily Farr, has died and recalls a firelight conversation "until our eyes fixed on each other;" in "The Pond," he takes pleasure in a lover's "breasts that rise and fall" as she breathes, but "Then I see mourners gathered by an open grave." The poem ends with a section called "The Cup" that suggests continuing epiphanies.

The realization of aging seems very often to relate somewhat to the "unchanging age" Levertov suggests we all hold on to, thereby producing, sometimes, a comic (or at least ironic) view of the body. Robert Creeley directs a poem to his body called "Oh," in which he deals with flesh that sags, brittle bones and the "flaccid change/ of bodily parts," and finally asks for "some sign/ I'm still inside."

And Daniel Hoffman in a poem called "Jogger" deals with bodily changes in the aging person--the thicker nose, the "skin on the chin...[that] hangs down," and, dealing with the sort of self-imagination defined by Levertov, he tells us that within sight of the finish line, "His record is writ in flesh."

In our age poets have supported themselves to a large extent by serving on English faculties at universities and consequently have become appallingly aware, by contrast with their students, of the onset of the scarecrow syndrome, which often involves linguistic change as well as cultural. William Sylvester in a poem with a long title (that is almost a poem in itself) deals with an attempt to use a youthful locution: "A Student Wrote/ Reeks of Joy/ Can you Believe it/ Reeks of Joy/ What Do They Learn in High School These Days?" The poem realizes the locution through an historical examination of self insights, including erotic semi-fantasy.

Disintegration or decay is another aspect of the scarecrow poet's baggage. Leonard Nathan in a third person poem called "Old Poet" creates a writer who seems to have had a share of Ezra Pound's influence and who gets "smaller/ each year, more Japanese." He is happy with one pine tree "and the mossy rock in its shade." His typist is older than he and "makes three more mistakes/ each poem" that he is too shy to complain about. His only issues are "the beginning and the end." His pleasure seems to lie in being able to grasp his ultimate end.

Realization of one's decay demands a sense of irony and the comic that sometimes reaches the near outrageous. Consider W.D. Snodgrass in a poem called "An Envoi, Post-TURP." His epigraph deals with a side-effect of the procedure: "After Trans-Urethral Resectioning of the Prostate, men experience retrograde ejaculation, the semen being passed later during urination." The poem opens with an allusion to Ben Jonson's "On My First Sonne" ("Farewell, thou child of my right hand, and joy;/ My sinne was too much hope of thee, loved boy,..."). Snodgrass's conceit is that he has lost children through ineffective semen: "Farewell, children of my right hand and bliss./ You'll come no more but in bright streams of piss." And he develops the vicissitudes of a life of marriage, procreation, and (for want of a better term) child development, all of which are turned around by the surgery. But the TURP has had its effect and the allusions become Shakespearean, from *Hamlet*, and move in grand Spenserian fashion from pentameter couplets to a concluding pair of maledictory alexandrines.

Which leads us quite naturally to another category of subject matter that engages the scarecrow poet, love and sex. And it is here that the verse is most fraught with the comic, perhaps because it, like death itself, is so powerful a drive and creates such fears and anxieties that we must deal with it from the distance or inversion that develops with humor. Sex, of course, also involves us with other elements of our society via symbols. The car, for example, has often been associated with physical desire, and David Ignatow in his prose poem "43" from *Shadowing the Ground*, with quiet irony and rich humor, develops for an old man the teen-age symbol of "having wheels."

Hayden Carruth suggests that he has written so many poems about aging that he has "had to make an oath not to do any more," and he adds that many of his poems about aging "are also about sex, which...is natural." He tends to avoid the comic, preferring serious ironies. In a short poem called "A Backyard in California" he hears someone playing a dulcimer that provides "Cool tones on the hot noon air," and he is taken by the sunlight on palm leaves that provides a "tango for the eye," the sensuousness of the hot afternoon sunshine becoming of itself "sufficient."

And in a sonnet, "Pray You Young Woman," Carruth addresses a young mistress who he knows is having an affair with a young man. He accepts this but doesn't want to be reminded, being more able to "stand delay/ Better than that too clearly you'd betray/ My doting...." He admonishes her to "play the long bright day/ With his [rival's] young body" and come to him at night, letting his "decay" be masked in "perjury and mercy...."

These problems of the elderly have been with us and celebrated in verse at least since Ovid. As in the *carpe diem* genre, these aspects of scarecrow verse depend on the poet's making the realization new and finding new insights. John

Woods in a poem called "Playing" picks up on a childish notion, opening with "Once you said, could we play?" His young woman affirmed that "We can do anything we want." They did, but the end of the game is resolved in a childish locution as well.

The desires of the flesh always involve fantasy, particularly those pangs that we experience in our youth. But age as well can prompt the likes of Grace Butcher's "It's Finally Come to This," a poem that opens with "All my lovers now/ are made of air...," and then the lovers of a lifetime congregate in her fantasy, giving her the opportunity to "tell them/ everything that needs to be said/ that should have been said before." Fantasy grows as the poem develops and solid bodies "start to form around them," causing her, first, embarrassment in their meeting each other, and ultimately in having all the love she wants, "like it or not."

Barbara D. Holander in a poem called "Swimming Against the Tide" looks around her at the young women in a shower room with "nubile bodies..., thighs taut and tender" and asserts that "My markings are the flow/lines of the tides; inside/I'm firm as an apple." And she awaits "my last chance boy/ rising from the sea...."

Reality becomes fantasy, returns to reality and again to fantasy for William Sylvester in "Cockles by the Sea." While walking on the beach not far from Cannery Row, the poem's speaker sees a woman jog by him "in light blue Nikes" who grins, which he is not sure to take as "complicity" or "kindness" and which leads to the reality in fantasy of their perhaps having made love "ages ago and I forgot." The poem returns to reality.

Indeed, we also still have aging relationships something like the Brownings, though perhaps more real and, for us, more believable. Marjorie and Philip Appleman are, as the husband poet suggested to me, in "the best is yet to be" category. They both retired early from their teaching appointments to become full-time writers. Ms. Appleman defines a continuum in her poem "Love," in which the strength of her love is gauged by the strength of the stream of her husband's urination, which is "warm and healthy": a love image that encompasses the very real concerns of advancing age--the "healthy" stream is cogent in defining the comfort and fragility of a "Love,/ still going strong."

Her husband's poetry is also quite positive, while remaining bound to reality. In his "Anniversary" he suggests that the celebration is done rather with "drums and cymbals" than "violins," but the years have left scars--for him, one is in his hand and another along the arm, and he knows her "scars at midnight/ by touch." They've learned, he says, the "Pidgin language/ of the heart, just/ enough to get by on...," always making "it home, riding/ on empty." This imagery melds into the architecture of their lives, making the building of their relationship "plumb" and creating "secret passages/ leading to music nobody else can hear...," with promises of love still to be kept.

Memories are always a stock conceit, but a long life often provides many memories of people that one is perhaps not too keen on preserving. X.J. Kennedy's "Masquerade" defines this aspect of getting through the scarecrow stage by comically defining an escape from someone he would just as soon forget at a fortieth high school reunion. But this escape is not always pleasant, as Galway Kinnell suggests in the ninth section of an eleven part poem, "When One has Lived a Long Time Alone" (*When One has Lived a Long Time Alone*, New York, Knopf, 1990, p. 67.) When one has lived alone for a long time, he becomes misanthropic and suggests a modification of the Miltonic boast of Satan: "It is better to reign/ in hell than to submit on earth...."

But, of course, memory is an important aspect of one's experience and provides new experiences based upon one's time of life. Will Inman, who wrote that it "Shocks me to realize my birth year--1923--is closer to the Civil War than to 1991!" defines himself in a curious poem entitled "the virgin who remembers," as a person who "might as/ well be a virgin again. "His body has started to say no to him, and while he still has the memories, he is a "leftover" who cannot swap his memories for "fresh doings."

Certainly among the most poignant of the experiences of growing older is the loss of family and friends. John Woods, whose wife died in 1983, realizes in "How She Goes" that loss is common and must be dealt with--"Children need to know.../ the heart pains of fathers,/ the ways mothers become snapshots," and he is reminded of his loss by the presence of combs and boots.

One of the nation's most pressing problems, currently, is health care, and those past sixty, even if they are fortunate enough to have good health, are made aware at least once a year (when they take their physicals) of the persistence of the body's demeaning decay. Robert Creeley in a poem called "Age" defines the experience of a sigmoidoscopy or similar dignity-debasing procedure.

But perhaps more disturbing is the lapse of memory that Leonard Nathan deals with in "Left-Overs," where "Winter for the old/ is like opening/ the refrigerator sometime/ between midnight and dawn" and forgetting why you are there.

The experience of aging becomes surreal at times, as Alberta Turner suggests in "Parting Branches, Lifting Grasses." The poem opens with the assertion that being alone in the universe is easy: "only one self to compose, edit, read." But "Animals are more difficult. Words worry them." She has a talk with a cat that "explained in every inflection of miaow/ how she'd been turned out, chased, deprived." And when she gets to humans, she finds that "Women and men are hard, like holding a fistful/ of wires: every time I pull one, something/ it's not attached to jerks...." The last stanza contains a terrifying concession: "Admit it. I'm alone....The hand I shake's a glove./ Frogs don't know I'm there. Even eggs/ don't know I've eaten them."

Colette Inez in "Listening to Dvorak's Serenade in E" finds in the piece of music the concept of ripeness, where "oranges glisten.../ the apples have broken/ their juice in my mouth..." and she finds herself "alone at the edge/ of all the gold seasons...." The music shapes dancers, however, "on a bitter dust of roads" that ultimately lead to a prayer for vitality and comfort at the "shining harvest."

Many have suggested that all poetry is about death, and Donald Hall concludes that it is at least about growing old. Indeed, much poetry has been written about death by younger writers--it was a favorite subject of the Romantics and Victorians, as it was for the poets of the seventeenth century. But given the demographics of our century, we must view the subject matter from an expanded point of view.

Ignatow's entire collection, *Shadowing the Ground*, is comprised of old-age and dying poems; the poet is near eighty at this writing. In his poem "59" from *Shadowing the Ground* he asserts that he has "no compunctions" about death. "It Belongs to me," he writes, and while not personifying Death as does Donne in "Death Be Not Proud," he says that he and death speak with "the same voice" and "no one yet has told us apart." Furthermore, he "would have no compunctions" if death should tire of him; he would know that they had supported one another equally in "burdens" and "pleasures." The poem ends in a humanistic manner that parallels the traditional Christian ending of Donne's poem ("And Death shall be no more: Death, thou shalt die."):

> ...Death leaving
> shall deprive me of my life
> but then death too shall be deprived
> of being.

In poem "46" of *Shadowing the Ground* Ignatow makes real the perennial pun on death. It is a third person poem that begins, "Lying between her legs,/ he was performing an obeisance" toward the "transformations of his bones and body/ in regal time." The pun becomes metaphor as the lovers "heaved towards.../such pleasure as to obliterate.../ the knowledge of their future death."

I have been eclectic in my choices of poets and poems to illustrate what I define as scarecrow poetry, and I certainly have not in any way covered the range of what this poetry does--and does for us. But the poets and poems in this volume underscore the chief elements of the scarecrow genre in their art--wit, self-irony, humor, a sense of reality and truth, and a compassion for the human condition.

This essay and this book do not deal with a sociological problem, one that regularly attracts the attention of congressional committees. They relate, rather, to what men and women have always known about themselves but are now experiencing in another dimension. Pope suggested almost three hundred years ago that human beings were blessed in that "Heaven from all creatures hides the book of Fate,/ All but the page prescribed, their present state...." But now, indeed, we have experienced open heart surgery and know that if it works well and if colon cancer doesn't get us, we can look forward to a TURP (if we are males). The fear of Alzheimer's makes up for the fact that we perhaps have missed the terror of AIDS. Most of us don't die before we are done with sex, though the specter of sex being done with us is always at our backs. Add to this the possibility of terrifying loneliness and we have before us a very important part of the human experience.

We hope that this book demonstrates that our time has developed splendid scarecrow voices that sing and dance a celebration of our extended world for the poets themselves, the old in general, and for the younger men and women who can't escape.

--Robert McGovern

# Prologue

## Scarecrow

We pumpkins worship you. We orange globes,
harrowed in youth, hollow in our old age,
aspire to your straw. In the darkness
of our swelling and decay, in our days
of rook pestilence and the owl's blight
which scampers among the vines we spin in
furrows and the furbelows of weed, we
do you homage. All honor, Scarecrow! You
there, sunstruck, eminent among us, rag
lord of moonlight, crucified among stars,
sighted as none of us may be. The world
in which we root unrolls unendingly
beneath your gaze, furlongs your province.
We pumpkins worship you, we orange globes.

*I cannot see. Buttons for eyes, what would*
*I see? If I could hear, the crows' whispers*
*could tell me only of some simple fields,*
*potato-eyed and corn-eared, extending*
*to limits that would only barb my sleeve*
*and rend my cloth, if I could walk to them.*
*You worship me? a pole for a spine, a*
*timber for my extended bone, fingers*
*of hay stolen by wrens? I bleach and shake,*
*I shudder in the moon's dark. Pumpkins, crowd*
*of orange globes, I whistle in the wind.*

Scarecrow, we too would whistle in the wind.

--Lewis Turco

Marjorie Appleman

## Ode to an Old Woman Lurching Along Ninth Avenue

I move aside to avoid
your wavering walk to
nowhere
on thick, veined legs,
the uncertain rags on your back,
the dirty years
under your arms and between your thighs,
your barren shrieks of
longing.

And though your face gapes red
at me when you pass
only two feet away,
I pretend not to see.

I cannot bear to look my
self
in the eye.

## Love

She kissed him, pissing.
I love you, she said,
be careful when you leave.
The trickle paused: you
be careful, too.
Back in bed,
*Love*, she thought,
remembering gray whiskers
mixed with the black.
Love, she whispered,
hearing the trickle
warm and
healthy.
Love,
still going strong.

## Philip Appleman

### Sensual Music

*what is past, or passing, or to come*
*--W. B. Yeats*

You know that from day one you start
to lose a little of your heart;
your mother, with a world to save,
has given birth beside a grave,
and time, relentless surgeon's knife,
year by year trims off your life.
But moments teach you not to be
deceived by immortality:
it's far too little, far too much.
What you have is what you touch;
passion feeds on bread and bells,
a chime of sounds, bouquet of smells,
someone's arm around your waist,
the best desire you'll ever taste;
and every glance is one step of
the pilgrimage that leads to love--
silver voices, golden bough:
the immortality of now.

## Our Tree

When we dug it out, thirty summers back,
it wasn't as thick as a wrist, but it was straight,
symmetrical: a hard maple
with good genes.
Small as it was, with its little world of dirt,
it took four of us to lug it back
along the river bank, to shade
the shy grass at a brand new house.
Once in our ground, as the Bible says,
it was nothing but chattel:
we owned it.

Now paint is scabbing off the house,
and rust is cancer in the eaves again,
but the tree is tall and full
and tropically green. Two of us
who carried that sapling home
are underground forever; the other two
are going gray and making out their wills.
The maple sees it all: every spring
it takes a deep breath, puffs
a thousand wings, and murmurs in the breeze:
*There, you flesh-and-bloods who thought you owned me,*
*my seeds are dancing over fields and meadows,*
*and when you're lying low and making earth,*
*I'll send up sturdy shoots around your graves.*

## Anniversary

Maybe it wasn't strange to find
drums and cymbals where
there might have been violins, maybe
we couldn't have known; besides,
would it have mattered?
See what the years have left behind:
a thick scar in the palm of my hand,
a ragged one running along the arm.
And you:
I know your scars at midnight
by touch.

Everything we've learned, we've picked up
by ear, a pidgin language
of the heart, just
enough to get by on:
we know the value of cacophony, how to measure
with a broken yardstick,
what to do with bruised fruit.
Reading torn maps, we always
make it home, riding
on empty.

And whatever this is we've built together,
we remember sighting it skew, making it plumb
eventually, and here it stands,
stone over rock. In the walls
there are secret passages
leading to music nobody else can hear,
earthlight nobody else can see. And somewhere
in a room that's not yet finished
there are volumes in our own hand, telling
troubled tales, promises kept, and
promises
still to keep.

## New Year's Day

grabs you and yanks you forward: this
is no seduction, this is the rape
of tomorrow, next week, the blind thrust
up there ahead in the haze that is
the future, waiting
for one false move, one shiver
of desperate hope--then
the crystal dome shatters, and a random shard
trashes your dreams like a thug.
Now, before another minute
grips you by the shirt, now
is the time to count your mixed
blessings: that you get older and older
and older, every brawl
beefing up brawn, every fracture healing
to flint. So
you lob your resolution into the clouds--
you will take each sleet storm as it comes,
face into the wind, slog
through endless mud, and kick away one
disaster at a time. Every hour
your skin will be tougher, your eyesight
clearer, and on that final day, when
you have made the dazzling discovery,
you will call back joy to everyone:
all is well, all is well,
we are alone.

Russell Atkins

## Over His Dead Body

            of him:
milk in a years of sieved gush:
a threnody'd squawk of chickens
of hundreds squabbled to grocers from farms;
stiffened in hells of stoves--at last,
as trundled bones on plates that lair!
            --all this:
crack'd-apart of eggs, babes against
affrightful skillets glee'd by grease;
nameless butchers that pummelled
the gory steaks for abrupt of his fork
and teeth; unravelled bacon by the yard,
moving its char along his tubes,
could not be held, could not leave much;
oysters could not save a thing;
*nor* could shrimp from plundered shallows,
neckbones, heavy pork chops,
do much--nor could groundround
daunt; steamed up lobster,
lush'd with butter, failed completely;
the body no gravy could fill
to be morsel'd off to fat grubs.

Let my own personal feelings offend:
that he ate well enough we know

--as to what *end*--,

Robert Bly

## Orion in Fall

Orion, mourning, floats among the stars
Firmly...the farms beneath his feet.
How long it takes me to climb into grief!
Sixty years old, and still placing my feet
So hopefully each night on the ground.
How long it takes me to let ground go.
But that shameless man follows his dogs,
Hunting all night among the disappearing stars.

Grace Butcher

## It's Finally Come to This

All my lovers now
are made of air.

I turn towards them from where I sit,
address the air beside me
in all seriousness, tell them
everything that needs to be said
that should have been said before.

I'm getting used to this emptiness,
this lack of response, the ghostly touch
of my own arms around me.

Nothing could be simpler:
all this space full
of lost voices. In a way,
they're not lost at all.

Next thing you know, bodies
will start to form around them,
and I'll be embarrassed
at having them all meet each other,
compare notes, decide to settle in,
share me.

I guess I'll finally have
all the love I want,
like it or not.

## Hayden Carruth

### Crucifixion

You understand the colors on the hillside have faded,
  we have the gray and brown and lavender of late autumn,
the apple and pear trees have lost their leaves, the mist
  of November is often with us, especially in the afternoon
and toward evening, as it was today when I sat gazing
  up into the orchard for a long time the way I do now,
thinking of how I died last winter and was revived.
  And I tell you I saw there a cross with a man nailed
to it, silvery in the mist, and I said to him: "Are you
  the Christ?" And he must have heard me, for in his
agony, twisted as he was, he nodded his head affirmatively,
  up and down, once and twice. And a little way off
I saw another cross with another man nailed to it,
  twisting and nodding, and then another and another,
ranks and divisions of crosses straggling like exhausted
  legions upward among the misty trees, each cross
with a silvery, writhing, twisting, nodding, naked
  figure nailed to it, and some of them were women.
The hill was filled with crucifixion. Should I not be
  telling you this? Is it excessive? But I know something
about death now, I know how silent it is, silent even
  when the pain is shrieking and screaming. And tonight

is very silent and very dark. When I looked I saw
  nothing out there, only my own reflected head nodding
a little in the window glass. It was as if the Christ
  had nodded to me, all those writhing silvery images
on the hillside, and after a while I nodded back to him.

## A Backyard in California

Someone is actually playing a dulcimer
Not far from here,
Cool tones on the hot noon air.

And sunlight on the palm leaves in the sky
Is slenderly
Divided, a tango for the eye.

All is languorous. Old age
Is slow, the edge
Of shadow creeps, and lust and rage

Are the privileged only of the sun,
Which will go down
After the sufficient afternoon.

## Pray You Young Woman

Pray you young woman come to my bed clean
And that your lover's dregs be drained away.
Come not quickly but leave time in between.
I'm old and waitful, I can stand delay
Better than that too clearly you'd betray
My doting. True. Sweetheart, you must be mean
A little, devious and deceitful, and not say
You come from him--I'll know. Just go, obscene
As ever you wish, play the long bright day
With his young body; then come, draw night's screen
Over me, pleasure me, let my decay
Be hidden. For your hands can touch gangrene
    And make it seem like my green springtime still
    In perjury and mercy if you will.

## Tanck's Song About His Unicameral Mind

In May, was it, Ophelia drowned?
    Today the watery breeze blurred
a clump of tulips, tight-set and orange,
    as though it were a wavering
face. I fell asleep then

in the chair of my old age
    as I looked out. I remember
wondering when springtime had left
    the world. Years ago, no doubt.
The truth is I knew the lady well.

## Æolian

The musician late at night in his little house
    on the hillside, working. His gray hair tousled,
wispy curls. He wears a gray sweatshirt.
    To make it from the immediate sounds, from
nature, as he had been taught, and he listens
    to the wind in the obsolete TV antenna
which he always means to take down. An
    Æolian chord, the bent tines of the antenna
vibrating differently but in numbers, patterns
    of number. He writes them down for the
hundredth time. He gets up, lights a cheap cigar,
    sips his Metaxas from a shot glass. He looks
out at the first light, at the dead dark grass
    on the field littered with winter's branches,
the moon paling in the west. Upstairs his
    young woman, beautiful and enchanting, lies
asleep. It is Easter morning. They love the
    holidays, being sentimental, the ritual
occasions, and certainly in earlier
    incarnations their souls had been devout.

Last night they gave one another Easter
    baskets with eggs and candy and made love

and said it was a holy day indeed for them.
    Indeed. Is that the music? What's to be put
to use? Humming to himself, a rhythm, the slap
    of his car on the tar-ridges of the interstate,
so trite. The Æolian harp is on top of his house,
    sitting up there, a vulture randomly twanging.
Nothing beautiful. No meaning. Not even
    interesting. He scuffs his hand through his hair.
"In order to use it you have to put it in something,
    you have to invent something around it. What?
Only oneself, over and over." His cigar is
    bitter, he throws it in the cast-iron stove,
a puff of blue smoke emits from the firebox,
    his eyes water, he presses his palms against
his cheeks, forcing his mouth into the shape
    of a sucker's, his face looks like a mutilated
starfish, he falls on the sofa, that gray reef
    just under the water where the Æolian
intervals are muted, distorted, but still
    audible, and he slides into his angry sleep.

Albert Cook

## The Poorly Shielding Parents

The poorly shielding parents have passed away.
Behind the very hospital
where my father died, outbuilding
residences have been laid out along a circular drive
where at staggering cost
in evergreen-shaded cubicles of brick,
they tend the dying.

Nuances gone, the living man
who has lost the recognition
to see I am reaching to let him know
he opened for me the doors
of all differences, is nodding,
mortgaged to an inaccessible memory,
lodging and sleeping in a wobble
the full life could not abide.
Vague faces and crowding trees
even each other out.
His elders could have been a handle
could he still flex, but they in the nature of things
are also long gone anyway
hooting and hooing in some great divide
as though foretold foreclosed
in a comparable no tomorrow.

If he mounts waveringly
the integers of sight,
they are backed by another blindness.
On good days it takes him a good
hour to get into a book
he sped through when his eyes

were not slotted.
The hour never comes.

I have reached an age where the words of my coevals
are graved on stone in public places.
Those further on have moved on out of such reach.
I am still free to drive away and remember.

## Jane Cooper

### My friend

Sylvia said: *When I was younger--*
*you know how in the work of most composers*
*a single line dominates, the melody line?--*
*Well, years ago I'd think only about my daughter*
*or only about my marriage, about how to sing,*
*what Freud meant or some friend...But in Bach,*
*every voice is equal, each line has invention.*
*That's how it is for me now, life and death are equal,*
*I'm neither going up the hill nor down....*
                              She paused, then extended her fingers
like Landowska addressing the keyboard. *But I don't know,*
    she broke off,
*whether I'm making myself clear....*

### Childhood in Jacksonville, Florida

What is happening to me now that loved faces
are beginning to float free of their names
like a tide of balloons, while a dark street
wide enough only for carriages, in a familiar city,
loses itself
to become South America?

Oh I am the last member of the nineteenth century!
And my excitement about sex, which was not of today,
is diffusing itself in generosity of mind.

For my mind is relaxing its grip, and a fume
of antique telephones, keys, fountain pens, torn roadmaps,
old stories of the way Nan Powell died
(*poor girl!*) rises in the air

detached but accurate--
almost as accurate
as if I'd invented them.

Welcome then, poverty!
flights of strings above the orange trees!

## The Blue Anchor

The future weighs down on me
just like a wall of light!

All these years
I've lived by necessity.
Now the world shines
like an empty room
clean all the way to the rafters.

The room might be waiting for its first tenants--
a bed, a chair, my old typewriter.

Or it might be Van Gogh's room
at Arles:
so neat, while his eyes grazed among phosphorus.
A blue anchor.

To live in the future
like a survivor!
Not the first step up the beach
but the second
then the third

--never forgetting
the wingprint of the mountain
over the fragile human settlement--

Robert Creeley

## Age

Most explicit--
the sense of trap

as a narrowing
cone one's got

stuck into and
any movement

forward simply
wedges one more--

but where
or quite when,

even with whom,
since now there is no one

quite with you--Quite? Quiet?
English expression: *Quait?*

Language of singular
impedance? A dance? An

involuntary gesture to
others *not* there? What's

wrong here? How
reach out to the

other side all
others live on as

now you see the
two doctors, behind

you, in mind's eye,
probe into your anus,

or ass, or bottom,
behind you, the roto-

rooter-like device
sees all up, concludes

"like a worn out inner tube,"
"old," prose prolapsed, person's

problems won't do, must
cut into, cut out...

The world is a round but
diminishing ball, a spherical

ice cube, a dusty
joke, a fading,

faint echo of its
former self but remembers,

sometimes, its past, sees
friends, places, reflections,

talks to itself in a fond,
judgmental murmur,

alone at last.
I stood so close

to you I could have
reached out and

touched you just
as you turned

over and began to
snore not unattractively,

no, never less than
attractively, my love,

*my love*--but in this
curiously glowing dark, this

finite emptiness, *you, you, you*
are crucial, hear the

whimpering back of
the talk, the approaching

fears when I may
cease to be me, all

lost or rather lumped
here in a retrograded,

dislocating, imploding
*self,* a uselessness

talks, even if finally to no one,
talks and talks.

## Funny

Why isn't it funny when you die,
at least lapse back into archaic pattern,
not the peculiar holding on to container
all other worlds were thought to be in--

archaic, curious ghost story then,
all sitting in the familiar circle,
the light fading out at the edges,
and voices one thinks are calling.

You watch them go first, one by one,
you hold on to the small, familiar places,
you love intently, wistfully, now
all that you've been given.

But you can't be done with it
and you're by no means alone.
You're waiting, watching them go,
know there's an end to it.

## Oh

Oh stay awhile,
sad, sagging flesh
and bones gone brittle.

Stay in place,
aged face, teeth,
don't go.

Inside and out
the flaccid change
of bodily parts,

mechanics of action,
mind's collapsing
habits, all

echo here
in mottled skin, blurred eye,
reiterated mumble.

Lift to the vacant air
some sigh, some sign
I'm still inside.

## Robert Dana

### Anniversary

*for Liz*

I lose track of myself.
Today is the same day,
July 22nd, Dillinger was
shot to death, in 1934,
by federal agents, under
the lights of the marquee
of the Biograph Theatre
in Chicago. And this
morning, another cold,
Dillinger rain is falling.
Like you I no longer
remember what movie was
playing; or, if I ever
knew it, the name of the
woman in the red dress.
On my radio, violins
are jabbering and raving.
And the rain's talking
again, in its millions
of little tongues to the
bright leaves. Across
Westview, in the garage,
the minister's kids are
reinventing the world
as a para-sail. And I'm
trying to recall exactly
the tone of your voice
as you say, "Everything
happens more slowly
where I live. Even
falling takes a long time."

## Salt

There's so much to forget.
I've never been one of your
rememberers. Maybe because,
when I was young, nothing
stayed, or I was always moving
on. I was alone, as I am now
at this table, wiping clean
this cheap Danish stainless
with which I ate; twisting
and tearing this two-day-old
crust of sourdough; wiping
up the last breath of dressing
from the plastic dish; salt,
vinegar, and oil on my tongue.

## Madeline DeFrees

### Mai-tai Music

Gazebo for a grandstand, the band plays island songs
while hotel guests sip cocktails
round the pool. The leader says, "I'd like to
introduce my husband, the founder of the band."
She curls his fist around a mike,
locks fingers with his ringed left hand. "We've been
together 30 years."

                And now he's almost blind, one
eye, opaque and squint, and one
unfocussed in a face of stone. Something's not right
about his gait. He stands or sits, awaiting
unseen signals, his look lobotomized. "This is real
good therapy for him." She pries her fingers
loose, both hands pleading

                on the mike, and sways her
hips, perhaps reminding him to smile. The knuckles
of her right hand graze his cheek.
His face stays set. She smiles for both of them.
*All I have to offer you is me*...The catatonic
syllables of lyrics in his head
escape his lips as if the music were a walking stick.

Returned to morning cold, the melody dead, guests
find the sun a myth to live with
until it goes down. Only the words linger on,
drifting like snow in the head. They remember
the words when their singular lives
touch down and the hand joined to theirs in the end
is the hand of the paid provider.

## A Visitor's Guide to the Lewisburg Cemetery

Not a sparrow falls...and my heart takes off
into another country. The heaven or nothing
writes a vapor trail over the river
vault. The riddle Shelley hoped to crack
that time with Jane Williams
when he talked of tipping the boat--"Now
let us solve together the great
mystery!"--and Jane got out to wade ashore.
The cryptic figures chiselled on stone
by the body's weather. *Your number is up*,
the saying goes, and the dice, like the gun
in Russian roulette, already loaded.

Finding my way through the graves to the
church and not the reverse, I come
to the granite slab marked FEINOUR. And yes,
I say, it's as good as any, a faint
wind skewing black oaks on the hill
overlooking the steeple. Moss and tendril
already creeping into my legend: *November 18,*
*19-19*--repeating digits, a tic
in the temple. In the space of a hyphen
characters soften, the tool in my hand,
a power drill running away with the motor,
carving the fatal numbers.

In this leaptide the paired 8's balance on
their torsos, and needle-thin,
the obelisks raise acronyms above the crowd.
Amid a clutch of verticals, I call
that horizontal man the Sleeper of the Year.
His landlord neighbor runs
lead-pipe around a plot to keep the vagrant
footsteps out. Cold light breaks through.
When a cardinal whistles

low in my ear and a skylark answers, I know
this is all in the head I am out of
here in the hectic west wind of the graveyard
wandering out-of-the-body.

## Spiritual Exercises

*Knees up*! Sophie shouts. We're jogging in place,
one mild gigolo and a pool full of women--
teens to seniors--with every physique
in the book. Madison Avenue gods call our drill-
sergeant a Full Figure. I call her
*No Jiggles*, read *solid state*. Strong as a
tugboat with plenty of
cargo in tow, she's pulling us through
holy routines: Little-Engines- clenching weak
ankles -That-Could- tie themselves in
French knots.
        *Flat on the bottom*! Sophia yells at
our feet, her short blond cut
unruffled as the blue cool of ecstatic eyes.
Is it *my* bottom or the pool's? I can't
see through the roily water past the hard rock
drowning out measured
instruction. Just when I'm sneaking a look at the
hour, she tells us to do
Pendulums. Elbows flexed, lifted high, my lower arms
sweep inward and out: Grandmother Clock in
brassy precision.

        Tanned statuesque, the Amazon
goddess floats her breasts on water
I try not to swallow. Birds flutter from nests of
Mother Wren's arthritic fingers. When music turns
mellow I know that we're cooling down to
the moment for gliding: *left, swoop, pointed toes,*

*wrists leading the body* to
paradise-under-the-shower. *Ole*! I say, meaning
Oil-of-, fighting the locker room bull,
lathering supple attachments. A long stretch for the
beach towel, heavenly clothes.

R.P. Dickey

## At a Concert

*--for Frank Cedrone and Victoria Markowski*

They hold everything together
As they play, the husband-wife
Duo-pianists, famous, getting through
Long complicated sonatas and rondos.
This involves them and such excellence.
No, this is about me. Or them.
They play. They are around sixty.
I'm around sixty, again and again
In this eternity each of us choose.

They're up there now with their heroes.
Once they were children, practicing.
This is what I was thinking.
Once they were children, practicing.
This is what it has all come to.
They play Clementi, Chopin, Liszt.
This is what it has come to.
This is a life. I know them. I weep.
Once they were children, practicing.

## Keeping the Crows Away

The scarecrow
In the field
Smiles as the crows
Peck the corn
He guards
And he wades
(The water up to
The zipper of his
Denim cutoffs)
In the river
Of dreams near
The old tower
Only a little
Rickety where
The princess
With a platinum
Tip on one tooth
Lives as he
Looks at her
The straw in his wig
Twitters she
Looks at him
Forever
And the crows
Fly away temporarily.

John Dickson

## Confession

When I think of the time I have killed,
the days I have murdered--
some that died easily--
days like phlegmatic fish that were ready to die,
days like sluggish birds
that would otherwise have been prey for cats,
tired, exhausted days like ponderous, rotten trees
or old dogs with sleep in their bones.

But even vital and lively days I have murdered,
stepped up behind them when they were their happiest,
at the peak of their vigor,
and slipped my knife of fine-tempered boredom
between their ribs
and watched with no emotion
as they slumped to the ground.

And often,
usually in the cold grey of winter
or when rain came as a depressing drizzle,
I would take a day up to my apartment
and we would have a snack and talk
and listen to music
and then we would stretch out on the studio couch
still talking and thinking
until I, sometimes against my will,
would hold a pillow over the day's face
until all breathing stopped.

Some days died hard--
days I would ply with liquor and bludgeon to death
or poison with special emotions I had developed.

Some I even starved to death,
locked them up in parlors of puritan Sundays
which became stone towers
with moats of abstinence around them
and let them rot with television and bridge.

The days of summer I treated most gently.
I would always choose one of exceptional beauty
and we would lie for hours on the warm beach
turning slowly, slowly,
facing the orange sun as it moved through the sky
and then, just before dusk,
I would suggest that we go for one last swim
and we would step into the cool water
and wade past the breakers
and swim out, out past the sandbars and buoys
to a spot as deep green as dark moss
and we would tread water for a few moments
and look up at the first star
and then, as the last trace of color drained from the sky,
I would press the day's head down under the waves,
waiting until the bubbles stopped showing
before I would swim back to shore alone.

Of course there was some remorse at first--
in autumn with its anguish of leaves turning brown
or in winter with its finality of ice--
when I would think back with a sense of loss
for all the beautiful days I'd destroyed,
though lately such qualms no longer disturb me.

But I know I'm almost finished;
there is not much time left to kill
and there are fewer days that I care to murder.
Besides, I have been so careless with these crimes--
someone is certain to find the skeleton
of a murdered day wedged between the rocks

or the hand of a mutilated day
protruding from the ground
with some incriminating clue nearby,
like my glove or my comb or the print of my shoe,
and I will be apprehended at last
and locked up with days and days and days
that will sooner or later
torture me to death.

<u>Anne Fasulo</u>

## Make-Over

She strokes across my forehead, smooths
down by the nostrils, the upper lip,
her young fingers carefully apply
a liquid base, the right shade to hide
the old spots, the worry lines, bumps.
She gives my skin a finished look,

matted, as in still life.
She leans toward me, I look through
a skein of loose hair, straw-gold,
a Rumpelstiltskin color, as mine was
when I was nineteen. I close my eyes
for shadow, sunrise pink or deepwater

green, pressed against the lids
by the same soft fingers that play
the piano, Mozart, Marvin Hamlisch.
She outlines the eyes, darkens the lashes
with a steady hand, drawing me a melancholy
glance of longing, an Ingrid Bergman.

I suck in my cheeks, she finds
the cheekbone, sorts through
her magical bag of tricks for blush,
uses hers. I don't have any.
My blushes have disappeared
with middle age. I am ready,

having waited at ease
under daughterly hands, feeling
again the tiny place, the soft spot

of her, little blonde ponytails
tightened with rubber bands, ribbons

to match a polka dot dress.
She has a forgiving touch, smooths
away the mistakes, teaching me
about make-up and the textures of love.

Stuart Friebert

## This Time in Our Lives

We're watching Sophocles in Athens.
It's your first evening out since deciding
on a wig to hide the effects of radiation.

The Greeks got it right. Black wigs for
tyrants, blond for heroes, red for comic
servants like Danny Kaye. The early Church

did its part, frowned on wigs as evil.
Along came Louis XIII, prematurely bald,
so back they came again. From *perruque*

to *periwig* to *wig*, we shorten as we lengthen.
In one of our books, I see the 18th Century
produced more than 40 types: pigeon's wig,

comet, spinach seed, artichoke, wild boar's
back--moving freely among flora and fauna.
Some women owned them all in different tints.

Shaving off our own hair, donning that of others
is right up there with Pepys, whom we've taken
to reading at this time in our lives. He wore

his own hair for a wig! But I still can't
fathom this: when we confess our sins, you in
yours are more guiltless than the rest of us.

God must know that. I turn back the covers,
take you in my arms. Wait, you say, Nobody
kisses me in my wig, and toss it clear across

the room. I'm the sort of fool you're making
me out to be. When I wag my head all the world's
a stage again. You know what's about to happen.

## Cremation Thoughts

The box of ashes the funeral home
signs over to us hits us with its
weight. We pass it back and forth
in a bewildering tempo. The ashes
seem to spread before the mind's
eye. It's as if the air changed,
and all you believed had vanished.

If you take them to the mountains
where I know she wanted to rest,
the funeral director says, Make
sure no one's around. The first
policeman who sees you will arrest
you. It's the law. We nod and help
each other on with our coats, make
for the car. The little tree we stop
by seems so bare you tie a yellow
ribbon to a branch. We let Dad take
the box by himself to the gulley
beyond, watch him broadcast like
some Johnny Appleseed. It's normal,
I suppose, to wonder what we'll want
to do with our remains, but this
hardly seems the time to say much.

Some people approach now, coming
energetically along the trail through
the narrow canyon, the great rock walls
rising around them. They stop right
past us, talking excitedly together

in what seems to be Navajo. They're
quite out of breath. Mom's emphysema,
I think, that's not what it was like,
I know. But it wanted something from
her she couldn't give and I start to
drift, through the slow ride back down
past cactus having a hard time of it
this year. At the house, I wake up in
anger, with a firm resolve to be buried
in what's left of me, won't even bother
to look up cremation in the O.E.D.

## Robert Funge

### Three Trees

One red cluster
of leaves at the top of a tree outside my window,
by its side
bare to its lower branches the same size tree
clings
coldly to a dozen dark brown leaves.

Makes me wonder
if I'll die from the bottom up, the mind clear
fierce and red
as the center maple, or barren at the top,
witless
and dark, rageless and cold.

On the other side of the red-topped tree
a third maple
shed wildly all at once with the last fierce wind.

### The Old Man of San Carlos

An old man sat, remembering.
A wrinkled little boy, smiling
with just the faintest trace of something
on the corners of his mouth.
He stared as if to occupy
the space he stared at with the past.
The cold curved modern bench betrayed
the vision that his memory made;
and when at last his gaze replied
he blinked, and saw the new parade.
Short skirted girls stirred

only his memory now.

The old man heard the bells of noon,
and started off with slower feet
than started off at other noons
on other walks down Laurel Street.
He walked a ways, and he felt blest
that there were no more hills to climb;
but pampering his tired feet
he stopped to rest, and smell a flower,
and watch a butterfly, and think
of how man's tampering with time
had given him an extra hour
to watch his shadow slowly shrink.

The old man sat of afternoons
in Burton Park, on benches that
were old as he, peeling and gray
where green had been, and he would see
with vision blurred small children play.
He kept his counsel with the squirrels,
and laughed his almost silent laugh
remembering how small boys and girls
would run to him when he had half
these years on him; and then he blinked
a tear, knowing that time would bring
an end to his remembering.

Ann Goldsmith

## Vanishing Point

Who will remember me after I'm dead?
I, an old woman
who struggles head bent
over tree roots
hauling my swollen heart
like a carcass
toward some child's line
drawing of horizon?

Who will wash me and fold my hands?
Wear my rings?
Pack up my shoes and poems?
In that last moment
will I gasp out a name
no one can recall?
Why weep today
for the blue soldier doll,
the garnet beads,
the hairs on a man's forearm?

When the forest and the small room
run together, who will
sing me out from under the trees?
Open the river and let me in?
Ah me, the questions
of an old woman
trouble no one but herself
and one or two scrubby hills
more rock than grass.

## Bequest

The new face grew like a mushroom,
soft, white, secret
under leaves, overnight.

One day it was there,
jowled, with large irregular brown
spots and eye pouches.

Had there been rain the night before?
The moon had rubbed itself
on the usual urns and bedposts,

the shadows met as always
under porches, behind knees.
She had slept well, no

dreams. Not even
long black trains or a wing of ice
where the road curves.

Yet here it was, this face,
a student effort
if ever she saw one.

She recognized the jowls:
they belonged to her grandmother,
who wore the spots on her hands.

The skin she found friable,
seamed with small broken tracks
like used wrapping paper.

Two small puff adders
dozed
under the eyes.

This face could not belong to her.
Let the fairies come for it,
hang it from some old sycamore.

She'd scare up another out back
after dark, smooth
as snake oil, inscrutable

as the smile on water,
rune-eyed riddle
of rhymes and far-off tunes.

That would do to go on with,
to cross the next field
and then the river.

## Mac Hammond

### Golden Age

What's an old man like you doing
In *The Garden of Love,* Venus, Adonis
Dallying, nymphs and swains in postures
Of amor, dripping rivulets and reeds.
Alessandro Scarlatti, you can't fool me
With your classical allusions--I know,
At the beginning of my own old age,
That your neighbor's daughter inspired
Your serenata, her plump breasts,
Because, when I first heard the lift
Of this music--trumpets, two sopranos,
Strings--it was like meeting (what in
the) another st-stunning young face.

Doris Headley

## Hipbone

I have not been so close
to my bones for years,
swathed as they were
in disguising flesh,
their shape and size
a hidden mystery.

Surgery pared me down
to this new knowledge
of comforting density
that belies the enemy
at work in my cells.

This hipbone neatly curves
into my grateful palm
like a secret handshake,
like ball to mitt.
I may even eschew cremation
for the sake of this
sweetly sculptured bone.

William Heyen

## At Times Square on My Birthday

A children's gospel group from Brooklyn (where I was
born)
sings "Amazing Grace" on the corner of 43rd
for wretches like me afraid

of "all eternity." Here, night falls later, but falls.
Not that signs blink off, not that moonbeams
do or don't stream down.

We measure night in this place not by light, or noise,
but by time's slowing in the mainspring
of a cop's watch, a wino's pockets

of purple blackness: during the slowing, I stop, turn twice,
& then again. A watch weighs more when wound--
I know my science.

A knife plunges into me, but mind quickens to heal the
wound.
I drink a bottle of medicinal dandelion wine
beneath a billboard blonde

with her legs spread. O lord, O city, for a few bucks
Anyman can time her movements on screen,
& shudder, trying to touch her,

trying to reach center. May your cherubim choir
keep me company on my fearful corner
until I sing, & come.

## The Ash

"Every minute, every day,
I hate this life.
I hate the trees, I hate the sunsets,
I hate my wife."

A nurse entered the room,
handed my friend his medicine,
a cup of water and two pills,
lithium and thorazine.

Eyes glazed, sedated,
but fists clenched above his sheets:
"I hate the doctors, the meals,
the beds, the stupid illiterates

who work here." I nodded,
but tried to save myself, ignored him,
closed my eyes, thought (for this was May)
of my mountain ash in white bloom,

at home, where I longed to be,
within its perfume-menstrual smell,
pure love mixed with death
mixed with pure swill

mixed with its own being
where, toward our earth's distillate,
airstreams of bees glide maddened
for blossoms of white filth,

thought of hands dipped
into cavities of ambergris,
of tongues licking scented necks,
lips sucking pus, maggots

humming their hymn of blue flame
in a dead animal's lung,
of the rainbow glaze of mucus,
the milky beauty of pond-scum,

of my own oval of flowering ash
in evening air, those powers that sustain
my body's sick-room odors,
the twisted smiles, the sunlit skin

cancers, the hate-vapors drifting
toward my broken friend, who cried
"I hate books, I hate the seasons,
I hate children, I hate the dead."

Where, if ever, will this end?
My friend moves from one ward to another,
embedded, circling lower. For now, outside,
I circle closer to the white ash flower.

## Daniel Hoffman

### Stop the Deathwish! Stop It! Stop!

--at least until the 21st century
because the present is too good to lose
a moment of--I would begrudge the time
for sleep, but dreams are better than they used
to be, since they enact the mystery
that action hides and history derides.
The past drains from the present like the juice
of succulent clams left in the noonday sun.
I spent the better part of my long youth
prenticed to arts for which there'll be small use
in whatever work the future needs have done:
I can file a needle to a point
so fine it plays three sides before it burrs,
or split a hundredweight of ice to fit
the cold chest with a week's worth in two blows;
is there many a man around who knows
by rote the dismantled stations of the El,
or that the Precinct House in Central Park
was once a cote from which the lambing ewes
and spindly lambs and crookhorned rams set out
to crop the green? In one-flag semaphore
I can transmit, or signal in Morse code
by heliograph such urgent messages
as scouts and sappers a boyhood ago
squinted through binoculars to read.
I still can cobble *rime royale* by hand
--and may, though now, about as few use rhyme
as wigwag or sun's mirrored beam to spell
their definitions of the ways that Time
endows the present it consumes, or tell
how only in this moment's flare we dwell
save when Memory, with her hands outspread,
brings back the past, like Lazarus, from the dead.

## Jogger

Entered in an event
For which he hasn't trained,

His body is pushing beyond
The limits of the body:

That flat, muscular stomach
So many sit-ups drew taut

(But his sweatsuit is shredded by moths)
Swags over his belt in a bulge.

And what's going on with his features?
They each have a will of their own.

They've decided they're not fully grown,
They're getting too big for themselves--

The nose is thicker, the skin
On the chin wants to hang, so hangs down.

And the face is creased and padded
In a parcel of furrows and folds.

Somewhere under addenda
Of belly and rump and jowl

Strides the crisp youth and slender
Who used to run a quick mile

As if he were still the same
Though what he ran toward became him.

He's within hail of the finish,
His record is writ in flesh.

Barbara D. Holender

## Swimming Against the Tide

Young women in the shower room
nubile bodies bending,
stretching, breasts and bellies,
buttocks, thighs taut and tender,
pliant as willow withes
you towel and buff.

You do not hear me singing
under my breath--
Oh, if you only knew
I am one of you.
My markings are the flow
lines of the tides; inside
I'm firm as an apple.

Once I kissed a prince
into a frog. He cursed me.
Entranced by your eloquent
young men who come
to borrow coffee, admire
your shining floating hair,
whisper diamonds are forever,

I wait for my last chance boy
rising from the sea
shrivelled and scaled
to gather my rosebuds
while he may.

## David Ignatow

### 43

I don't know which to mourn. Both have died on me, my wife and my car. I feel strongly about my car, but I am also affected by my wife. Without my car, I can't leave the house to keep myself from being alone. My wife gave me two children, both of whom, of course, no longer live with us, as was to be expected, as we in our youth left our parents behind. With my car, I could visit my children, when they are not too busy.

Before she died, my wife urged me to find another woman. It's advice I'd like to take up but not without a car. Without a car, I cannot find myself another woman. That's the sum of it.

### 46

Lying between her legs,
he was performing an obeisance.
It was his known self,
certainly not intended
to create a child, nor to make sex
the existence. There would be
transformations of his bones and body
in regal time, time that was this
thrusting towards the sadness
of climax within an aperture
of flesh, as she who lay beneath him
heaved towards what they sought
in common and that would bring them
to such pleasure as to obliterate,
at least for then,
the knowledge of their future death.

## 59

About death, I have no compunctions.
It belongs to me.
We speak with the same voice
and shake hands; we are so alike
no one yet has told us apart.

About death, I would have no compunctions,
if it should tire of me at some moment.
I would know we had borne each other
equally, our burdens equal
with our pleasures. Death leaving
shall deprive me of my life
but then death too shall be deprived
of being.

## Colette Inez

### Listening to Dvorak's Serenade in E

Everything has ripened,
the oranges glisten
in their sharp worlds,
the apples have broken
their juice
in my mouth,
I am alone at the edge
of all the gold seasons,
a tide of clouds
bearing me home
like a migratory bird.

And this bright music
shaping dancers
on a bitter dust of roads,
divining rods
that point
to a further distance:
stone, water, stone.

Dowser, find my deep stream.
Builder, make my house
to last in the ochre heart
of the falling sun,
in this shining harvest.

## Seven Stages of Skeletal Decay

0-5 Centers of ossification appear as I squall
"wyde in this world wonderes to hear."
The light my second amnion.
Mother like a frog, white exhausted thighs
precede my deciduous teeth, the better to bite
the asylum where I didn't earn my keep.
Ward of the state and stable criteria.

5-12 Acetabular elements join.
Ilium, ischium, pubis,
a little hen's breast against my hands.
In the corpulent dark hearing children grow
a song of bones as the moon climbed
and ovary bells, my eggs and the moon
tolling each month.

12-25 Epiphysial union of long bones.
Long bones in my stride,
glib nights, counterfeit smiles,
trumped-up charges against what I loved.
Years blindly eating childhood's fat.
Knowledge like a shield
wounds when pressed too near.

25-36 Active vault suture closing.
Active designs in the skull.
Delicate zippers sealing in
the stars, interstellar dust,
brackets of marriage, and one short birth
shaped like a comma between two worlds.

36-50 Lipping of scapular glenoid fossa.
Fossa, a ditch.
I have come to it.
Fossa, an abyss.
I wait for the master archeologist
to dig and pick,
tweezers plucking artifacts,
my trail of refuse and souvenirs.

50 Quasi pathological erosions of bone.
plus The pendulum's pit.
My old electrons blow their fuse.
Dark pond.
My mother like a frog,
white exhausted thighs collapsed.

plus What did it mean to play
a xylophone of bones?
An octave of stone. Delight. Decrease,
bleached lips dim against my fingers
closing in a stiffening fist,
dumb warrior
pitted against eloquent death,
illiterate mulch for those whose squalls
will go "wyde in this world
wonderes to hear,"
the light their second amnion.

Will Inman

## the virgin who remembers

if this keeps up, i'd might as well
be a virgin again. all those things i
used to do--happened in a previous
existence. i did them, they were done
to me, but now i'm shedding them like
old skin. i remember them the way i
recall a film i saw long ago once or
twice: i'm not sure how much is actual
memory and how much is just remembering
what i remembered from earlier yet. i
look back, and it's as if i'm looking
ahead to what will happen if i wait
long enough.
yet my body keeps saying **NO**
in more and different ways. i'm still
me, i guess, but i'm not the one who
still does those things, i'm the leftover
me who carries around memories i can't
swap for fresh doings. i can't even give
them away. who can carry secondhand
memories? who can live just to fulfill
someone else's fantasies. so i'm a virgin
sure enough, only i know what no virgin can
know. if i knew back when what i know now
--would i have ever done those things? i
think so. and more than i did. because i
wouldn't have believed then what i know now
even if i could've looked ahead and seen
into my now knowing. and i'd have stored
more firewood to burn on cold, lone nights.

## goat in a battered cage

how briefly we'd leave our polite middle-class
southern white world of the 1930s, how we'd
walk together into that kudzu thicket, hide
in its hummocks of vines, crawl under those
thick summergreen leaves, shed our clothes,
how we'd stretch our teenage bodies together
and kiss fierce, make motions that brought sky
sunless blue steep into the vines of our lithe
twisting flesh, how we savored that goat
between us, that glad sylvan god who laughed
in our mouths low with secret joy, how our
warm press of skin grew pagan into our souls,
found pagan already in our inmost trees,
waiting to be known.
        now you're dead.
                yet now
as i listen to Stokowski lead Bach's *Toccata*
and Beethoven's *Seventh*, those godfuried
sharings we grew later to love to, you're in
this room. i groan in my ribs to waken you,
o you waken in me, i cannot birth you but must
bruise this old self taking your young olive
body into my frayed substance, caught goat in
a battered cage, how you leap your grin across
my empty years, how you refuse to die, and i,
making room for you in me, only capture you
when i'd do better to let you set me free

## Josephine Jacobsen

### The Chosen

(*Grenada*)

The sick are coming the sick are coming!
Today is the healing of the sick. It is
today's Good News; there has been preparation.
In this church all the chairs have arms.

Brought by the strong, the sick will come in last.
Out there the beach is a perfect blaze; no normal
rainbow ever carried more colors than this Caribbean,
and the almond blossoms are blowing; they fall

on the sand, in the wind that wildly flattens
the candle-flames in their glass. Hibiscus
is seen through the brick-lace walls, red
as the little girls' barrettes: you could go on

with the sky, and their blue ribbons; and certainly
the clouds have the same white-white as their tall socks.
The faces, color of cocoa, obsidian, sand,
of bark, of nutmeg, are turned toward the door:

the choir, quiet, seethes with intention. Now!
Between two of the strong, the sick ones creep:
lame, mostly; enormously tough and fragile,
like dark, bent-over birds. Some

spectacular ravages; but sadly, largely
it turns out, the undramatic wounds of age.
They are lowered into chairs with dignity.
A tiny old woman chatters, chatters,

part prayers, part anecdotes to an
invisible friend. *Kumbaya!* the choir bays,
drowning the mocking-bird exulting
in health in the eucalyptus.

They lowered the leper through the roof, says the gospel,
because of the crowd. The lifted faces, intent,
savor this: part of the roof, right off--
and there is the leper! The next thing

you know, he has taken up his bed and gone
home. The faces are raised to that story.
They believe it could happen; did happen; but
will not, right now. The black tall priest

his sash embroidered with nutmeg bursting
through its mace, says he will bring them oil,
the oil of healing; and he does, bending, huge
and gentle. *Amen! Amen! It shall be so!*

shouts the choir: *hallowed be Thy name!*
*Amen! Amen! It shall be so!* It has a beat
like Carnival; is a kind of road-march:
the foreheads, the palms, are raised to the oil,

a huge wave lifts the entire place:
fronds that swing in the sun, the enormous
healthy day, the loud bird
in its tree. They are healed, healed:

they understand something I cannot:
that they wait: are loved: are in the palm
of the good power that chose their affliction.
*Pray for us,* the priest tells them, *You are closer to God.*

The bright chatterer pushes herself up
and begins to dance: a tiny road-march jump-up;
a Sister swirls, all veil and beads, to take her
claws, and down the aisle away they go like partners.

Now the Host rises, white and round
in the beautiful long black fingers
and even the choir is stricken
silent. Given: a new Body.

*Power! Kingdom!* shouts the choir
suddenly, *Glory!* The guitar goes
fast and deeper. *It shall be so!*
*It shall be so!*
The healthy leave first,

not to hurry the honored, in their slow
return to familiar sheets. If the terms of the contract
remain mysterious, it is signed. The chosen
wait in their chairs for those not chosen.

## Finally

Finally
the old woman saw

all things take back
their virtue

into themselves:

nouns swallow up
their adjectives;

the day's loose multitude
curl tight to now:

the whispering giant draw

into its acorn:
one ray compel

the starred abysses:
the gardens go into their

naked rose.

## Figure

Out of the bone landscape
of stone and sand, a man
on a burro appears

alone, distant;
egg for head, stick arms,
stick legs, out of all years

of the sand, the stone; going
to no seen spot, confers
a human form on the eye

before he vanishes
as though bony distance
had eaten him.

Nothing is like him. Vulnerable,
he has not profited
from the feral faunal data:

the yellow crab spider
on golden rod; the brown
beetle on soil; the katy-

did on its green leaf;
the delectable Viceroy
mimicking the acrid Monarch. Outwit,

or lie low and wait. The cock-
roach in 300 million
years has not seen fit

to change. Yet durability
cannot be said
to be all. Nor fear.

The stony bony sandy view
shifted itself, focused
upon him till he left it there.

Phyllis Janowitz

## Effects of Weather Conditions on One Woman's Frontal Lobes

After World War II the world was gray,
the earth covered over with ashes and winter.
Just rooming houses for us, boxed in, then

the long rains came and continued on.
If you want me to tell you what I know about this,
my niggling response is "I'm out of it"--

those forecasters' wimpy fears, another disaster...
I'd let trees and wind elect by motion what to say--
A slow-mo replay poked sluggish memory:

we were at a stultifying "football party"
in Michigan, everyone drinking draft beer
and Purple Passion, ice cubes in it. I said

*ice cubes!* and quit for good. These days I'm pleased
the lazy delivery wagons have speeded up. Feather-
bells are bountiful in summer. I hardly ever

need a rain coat. At one point I would have
lived anywhere regardless, I would have
loved anyone, but there was no one,

not then, not later, not ever; now when
monarchs arrive my pulse doesn't quicken
since it doesn't matter, there isn't any

matter to matter, no fist banging on
my heart trying to separate me from
habitual absences, my routine comas.

Let others' cleverness keep old windmills turning.
At present the burning question is what
to do with this perpetual sun.

## Wrapping It Up

The babies were fighting again,
hitting each other on the head
with coffee cans, shrieking. Some said
they were having fun. I was not.

War, war, everywhere, one cannot
go into the garden without
looking for trouble. What I want
is what is not, in life, my lot,

that's unacceptable. I'm not
acceptable. Acceptable
people speak to one another.
What's to say? Something, whatever,

speak. Monkey see. Monkey do. Who
among us is not a monkey?
Or crow? All summer we worry
about Elvis Presley. Does he

sing in some metaphysical
choir of birds songs pleasurable
as a chickadee's, but lonely?
All summer baby's been yawping.

His mother's tired of feeding him.
He is much bigger than she is.
Lazy. Everyone's out talking.
What you say is what you see is

what you want is what you get. I
want this summer forever plus
the crow, complaining. Freeze frame. But
we can't stay here. No trespassing

and we are. Corn fields, vacant lots,
the kneecaps of babies rubbed raw.
We are barely passing through. Not
through time, just a single summer.

Shirley Kaufman

## Yahrzeit

All day regret and appeasement flicker
in the memorial flame, long-burning candle
I light on the Hebrew date
when I remember, as variable
as the world is variable
for its wandering Jews.

I see him like a peddlar
under his sack, sandman, huckster,
itinerant lover returned
from the cold plot next to my mother,
some shabby motel-room Willy Loman,
to sell us what?

I wish I could find him
in the small flame, startled
and happy, reeling his catch in,
playing the big ones.
Whatever he knew about loss
he never told me.

When he was his own boss,
and his workers went on strike,
I called him the dirtiest word I knew:
*Capitalist*. I shouted and wept:
*You filthy capitalist*! We tried
to forgive each other.

There is so little to go back to.
Now that I'm edging toward the place
where everything happens
for the last time,

I need to hold him
in this cupful of night.

## On a Photograph of Myself as Grandmother

*for Samia and Sarah*

It's not a pose. They are so innocently
perfect against my arms,
though slightly unfocused.

I see myself sitting on the bench
between them in the sun
like someone I wanted to be.

I'm not ready. We are over-exposed,
our lips much paler
than they are,

the two girls already dissolving
in the hard light
that bleaches their hair

and drains the last color out of mine.
I am holding a book
wiped clean in the false radiance,

no print where my hand lies white
on the white page
and the children can't read yet

but they mouth all the words by heart.
I tell them again
how the lost bird looks for its mother,

an absence they almost
believe in, caught
in the middle of the book

where nothing is certain, listening gravely
to the sound a bird makes
when it's abandoned.

## X. J. Kennedy

### **Five-and-Dime, Late Thirties**

Your nose by frying franks'
    Salt pungent odor stung,
You'd perch a stool, give thanks
    For shreds of turkey strung

On a mound of stuffing doled
    With icecream scoop, lone spoon
Of gray canned peas, one cold
    Roll, cranberry half-moon.

The same recorded air
    Swung round the counters daily:
Once more, "Old Rocking Chair"
    Had captured Mildred Bailey.

Nearby, some lone gray head
    Lost in a dream apart,
Selecting glasses, read
    With slow lips from a chart;

Meanwhile, some rouge-cheeked jade
    In permanent spit curls
Pushed Maybelline eyeshade
    To adolescent girls.

At times a clanging bell
    Insistent as Big Ben
Proclaimed the news: some swell
    Had tried to change a ten.

On to the thick cheap pads,
    A last thin dime to blow,

To write new Iliads
    You'd steer course, even though

You longed for chocolates
    From the open-air glass case
Where, nightly, hordes of rats
    Shat in the licorice lace

As sure as FDR
    Had kept us out of war.
Until one day the Board
    Of Health padlocked the door,

Brown Shirts had seemed mere show,
    Hitler a comic wraith
Far off. What you don't know
    Won't hurt had been our faith.

## Masquerade

At the fortieth reunion of your high school class
You'll meet a few whose memories you'd bypass.
Show them no sign, but shrivel down inside
The unidentifiable armor of your hide.

## How to Know You're Old

You know you're old when, serving time in line,
At last you reach a lace-encrusted bride
And when you'd plant the kiss you had prepared,
She suddenly looks scared and turns aside.

Phyllis D. Kramer

## Older Woman's Lament

All cats are gray after dark
And seductive is our fur.
During the day we cope with harassment;
Small paychecks and discrimination endure.
We watch as men become distinguished
And see ourselves only growing old.
We must not take young lovers;
After dark we are supposed to be cold.

And now comes the ultimate loss,
The last hit below the belt.
It was seen as a male condition
Something a woman never felt.
Last night I cried in my bath,
My crowning glory it cannot be called.
I am no longer seductive after dark;
My pussy is getting bald.

Maxine Kumin

## Spring Training

Some things never change: the velvet flock
of the turf, the baselines smoothed to suede,
the ancient smell of peanuts, the harsh smack
the ball makes burrowing into the catcher's mitt.

Here in the Grapefruit League's trellised shade
you catch Pie Traynor's lofting rightfield foul
all over again. You're ten in Fenway Park
and wait past suppertime for him to autograph it

then race for home all goosebumps in the dark
to roll the keepsake ball in paraffin,
soften your secondhand glove with neat's-foot oil
and wrap your Louisville Slugger with friction tape.

The Texas Leaguers, whatever league you're in
still tantalize, the way they waver and drop.
Carl Hubbell's magical screwball is still
give or take sixty years unhittable.

Sunset comes late but comes, inexorable.
What lingers is the slender hook of hope.

Denise Levertov

## Evening Train

An old man sleeping in the evening train,
face upturned, mouth discreetly closed,
hands clasped, with fingers interlaced.
Those large hands
lie on the fur lining of his wife's coat
he's holding for her, and the fur
looks like a limp dog, docile and affectionate.
The man himself is a peasant
in city clothes, moderately prosperous--
rich by the standards of his youth;
one can read that in his hands,
his sleeping features.
How tired he is, how tired.
I called him old, but then I remember
my own age, and acknowledge he's likely
no older than I. But in the dimension
that moves with us but itself keeps still
like the bubble in a carpenter's level,
I'm fourteen, watching the faces I saw each day
on the train going in to London,
and never spoke to; or guessing
from a row of shoes what sort of faces
I'd see if I raised my eyes.
Everyone has an unchanging age (or sometimes two)
carried within them, beyond expression.
This man perhaps
is ten, putting in a few hours most days
in a crowded schoolroom, and a lot more
at work in the fields; a boy who's always
making plans to go fishing his first free day.
The train moves through the dark quite swiftly
(the Italian dark, as it happens)

with its load of people, each
with a conscious destination, each
with a known age and that other,
the hidden one--except for those
still young, or not young but slower to focus,
who haven't reached yet that state of being
which will become
not a point of arrest but a core
around which the mind develops, reflections circle,
events accrue--a center.
                A girl with braids
sits in this corner seat, invisible,
pleased with her solitude. And across from her
an invisible boy, dreaming. She knows
she cannot imagine his dreams. Quite swiftly
we move through our lives; swiftly, steadily the train
rocks and bounces onward through sleeping fields,
our unknown stillness
holding level as water sealed in glass.

## The Two Magnets

Where broken gods, faded saints, (powerful in antique
    presence
as old dancers with straight backs, loftily confident,
or old men in threadbare wellcut coats,) preside casually
over the venerable conversations of cypress and olive,
there intrudes, like a child interrupting, tugging at my mind,
incongruous, persistent,
the image of young salmon in round ponds at the hatchery
across an ocean and a continent, circling
with muscular swiftness--tints of green, pink, blue,
glowing mysteriously through slate gray, under trees
unknown here, whose names I forget because
they were unknown to me too when I was young.

And there on the western edge of America--home to me
    now,
and calling me with this image of something I love,
yet still unknown--I dream of cathedrals,
of the worn stone of human centuries.
Guarded by lions with blunted muzzles
or griffins verdant with moss, gateposts open in me
to effaced avenues.
Part of me lives under nettle-grown foundations.
Part of me wanders west and west, and has reached
the edge of the mist where salmon wait the day
when something shall lift them and give them to deeper
    waters.

*Bellagio, November '89*

Philip Levine

## My Father With Cigarette 12 Years Before the Nazis Could Break His Heart

I remember the room in which he held
a kitchen match and with his thumbnail
commanded it to flame: a brown sofa,
two easy chairs, one covered with flowers,
a black piano no one ever played half
covered by a long-fringed ornamental scarf
Ray Estrada brought back from Mexico
in 1931. How new the world is, you say.
In that room someone is speaking about money,
asking why it matters, and my father exhales
the blue smoke, and says a million dollars
even in large bills would be impossible.
He's telling me because, I see now, I'm
the one who asked, for I dream of money,
always coins and bills that run through my hands,
money I find in the corners of unknown rooms
or in metal boxes I dig up in the backyard
flower beds of houses I've never seen.
My father rises now and goes to the closet.
It's as though someone were directing a play
and my father's part called for him to stand
so that the audience, which must be you,
could see him in white shirt, dark trousers,
held up by suspenders, a sign of the times,
and conclude he is taller than his son
will ever be, and as he dips into his jacket,
you'll know his role calls for him to exit
by the front door, leaving something
unfinished, the closet light still on,
the cigarette still burning dangerously,
a Yiddish paper folded to the right place

so that a photograph of Hindenburg
in full military regalia swims up
to you out of all the details we lived.
I remember the way the match flared
blue and yellow in the deepening light
of a cool afternoon in early September,
and the sound, part iron, part animal,
part music, as the air rushed toward it
out of my mouth, and his intake of breath
through the Lucky Strike, and the smoke
hanging on after the door closed and the play
ran out of acts and actors, and the audience--
which must be you--grew tired of these lives
that finally come to nothing or no more
than the furniture and the cotton drapes
left open so the darkening sky can seem
to have the last word, with half a moon
and a showering of fake stars to say what
the stars always say about the ordinary.
Oh, you're still here, 60 years later,
you wonder what became of us, why
someone put it in a book, and left
the book open to a page no one reads.
Everything tells you he never came back,
though he did before he didn't, everything
suggests it was the year Hitler came
to power, the year my grandmother learned
to read English novels and fell in love
with *David Copperfield* and *Oliver Twist*
which she read to me seated on a stool
beside my bed until I fell asleep.
Everything tells you this is a preface
to something important, the Second World War,
the news that leaked back from Poland
that the villages were gone. The truth is--
if there is a truth--I remember the room,
remember the flame, the blue smoke,

how bright and slippery were the secret coins,
how David Copperfield doubted his own name,
how sweet the stars seemed, peeping and blinking,
how close the moon, how utterly silent the piano.

## February 14th

Awakening at dawn thirty-
six years ago, I see
the lifting of her eyelids
welcome me home. I can
recall her long arms en-
circling me, and I reach
out until the moment slides
into all the forgotten hours.
All the rest of our lives
the tree outside that window
groans in the wind. In other
rooms we'll hear other houses
mutter and won't care, and
go on hearing and not
caring until our names
merge with the wind. One
room, bare, uncurtained,
in a city long ago lost,
goes with us into the wide
measureless light. A tune
goes with us too. Hear
it in the little weirs
collecting winter waters,
in the drops of frozen rain
ticking from the eaves to
pool in the tiny valleys
of their making. Six weeks,
and the wide world is green.

## Soul

In Castelldefels we say, "There are four thousand souls
living in this village," not daring to omit even
the squat, gray haired captain of the Guardia Civil
or the trailer camp of Gypsies who thrive on a grassy plot
down by the tracks, the men who shine my wife's boots
while leering shamelessly up her skirt, the women
who beg at the tables of the open-air cantinas
in the public square, rolling their eyes and pinching
the borrowed babies until they bawl. As a child
I was embarrassed to implore the Lord to take my "soul,"
whatever that was, before I woke. I was five then,
living splendidly in a two-story house on the West Side
with fenced yard, heated garage, and a governess to tend
my brother and me, a Mrs. Morton, who professed
a faith in the afterlife and thought it charming
at bedtime to force the twin heathens to their knees
to recite her rhyming prayer, which we did only the once
as a circus act for company. Thankfully the Great Depression
saved us, and Mrs. Morton, caught pawning my mother's
rings,
went packing--with no references--into the larger Christian
world.
We moved, carless, to a dim, cramped walk-up behind
a used-car lot on Livernois. There my spiritual life
got a second start when I collapsed on the way to school
for no known reason and awakened staring up into the face
of a policeman with the improbable name of Officer
German.
The school nurse, while fussing with my pulse and staring
at her watch, solemnly announced I must be dead,
and my mother was summoned from work to take me home
in a Checker cab. That night I lay face up on the couch
groping for words that might stay the inevitable.
I was allowed by the spirits that rule in such affairs
to return to life disguised as a seven-year old

not yet fully aware of the beauty of women's legs
or the firm skin that stretched across their gleaming
    sternums,
though Marta--our boarder from Nazi occupied Vienna--
asked me into her room one night to sample her talcums,
her colognes and creams, and to try on her silk garments,
which I stubbornly rejected, only to bring on a storm
of Middle Eastern abuse--, a lost opportunity
I lived to regret. In the sixth grade, seated beside
a budding girl in pleated skirt and starched white blouse
I felt for the first time my present incarnation
taking hold, and though I fought it for days, though I
    begged
the unknown powers within me for relief, preferring
to remain rounded off and complete, the yin and yang
of the eleven-year old, it went on. Now the long torpors
could descend on me each spring. I became the object
and no longer the subject of my own sentence. When I
    asked
the inconstant stars that occasionally winked through
the dim air over Detroit for their guidance, they answered
in an indecipherable riot of words, Basque and Chinese,
which I alone could interpret. Thus the sudden flight
to Havana in 1947 in the hope of mastering
Latin ballroom dancing, my enlistment in the naval reserve
in order to acquire discipline and bearing, the marriage
to a fifteen-year old suburban delinquent. All of this failed,
just as the year on the night shift at Wonder Bread
and the diurnal sweats of the seven ovens failed
to rinse me of indignation. The surprise came when
on my twenty-sixth birthday while sober a grown woman
chose me, who was not sober, to father her children,
and together we embarked on a life we could call ours
in the village of Castelldefels in the year of our Lord
1965, where returning home alone on foot after a long day
of idling in the great cemetery of Barcelona, I shouted out

to the night sky, "There is that lot of me and all so
luscious."
And believed it. I believe it now, even though
the squat captain of the Guardia Civil goes on censoring
my mail, the dwarf barber sneers as he calls me Don Felipe,
the butcher hints I lack the *cojones* to take her sister,
and each night the sea tears at the littered coast, the wind
rages through the pines, and--except for us--all four
thousand
souls, some alone, some in pairs, huddle in their beds and
pray.

Duane Locke

## An Old Man at an English Pub in Tampa, Florida

The old man watches
a middle-aged man in a black felt hat,
multicolored shirt,
puffing on a king sized cigarette
and emptying a pitcher of beer
down a sagging throat.
The middle-aged man
wears highly polished brown cowboy boots.

The old man watches
the youth in their body shirts
that display tattoos of roses,
hearts, mermaids and mothers;
observes their cut-off, patched,
faded blue jeans
that reveal shorts colored cerise
as they toss darts at a target.

The old man
feels out of place
in this ersatz pub,
sitting there alone
in his zoot suit.

## Mordecai Marcus

### A Man of Experience

The girls clinging to boys in movie lobbies
care nothing that I have refused to age with the years:
Sweet girl-gallery of revolt or peace
against the poise nature has lent them,
their faces caressed
as designing chance
dangles their hair,
their breasts brave emissaries.
What are their boys but long-legged birds
scratching in marshes,
pecking at words?
What famishment could make a girl care
for such sand-pebbled candy?
Do these boys know
how to go treasure-diving
to the low-slung mysteries
where the world marries itself
in volcanic heat?
Are they shining enough to be a mirror
to the core of beauty?
Yet, when I look up
to where I would fly with their girls,
a scarecrow hovers in the air
where I thought I went on eagle feathers,
and the only feathers are spines
on my cactus heart.
My love told me
there was a man she loved
around those spines
and that he was a warm meadow.
My flight was a cold dream.
Love is here,

away from the sky of mirrors.
I have nothing to offer those girls.
Their men are the grassy world
each love must come down to.

## Refusing Codgerdom

Half-way down a long hallway,
I thought the safest way to make it through
was to wrap myself in a codger's hide.

So I mounted this disguise,
rounded my mouth for a jolly flow,
let my fists pound down on wincing shoulders,
my ears and jaws spread out a heh! heh! haw!

Next I winked at shifty goings on
rippling their crinkled silk
with fistfuls of stray fingers--
a rich world for everyone else
but for the codger a belly-load of skinny laughs.

Towards the end of the hall,
I reached to stroke the carpet of my beard
but instead my chin was a bare sexy thrust.

My gut was lean and proud,
my scrotum tight as a drum,
my phallus an armed atom bomb.

So I jerked every kink from my leaning form,
and standing tall I raced straight ahead,
wiping the syrup from my puffy jaws,
wolfing down every sight, every form
that codgers clutch only to vomit up.

Jack Matthews

## Old Men Should Not Write Poems

Old men should not write poems.
They ought to stand cussing in their pants
and marvel at the way the weather's changed
and mutter *Ruin!* in a senile trance.

Old men should lie about the past,
brag about those things that never were
and disapprove of how the young dogs act,
aware all pedigrees conceal a cur.

Old men should brood on excellence gone,
should mutter bilious caution at the young
who'll never understand their words, spoken
in the world's oldest-known unknown tongue.

Old men refrain from writing poems;
and hold them quieter than breath,
too private for society or friends,
too public for the ear of death.

## The Party

Just because you leave the party doesn't
mean the party's over, of course, but it
might just as well be over, because it'll
be over for you; and it's not in the least
surprising that sometime shortly
before you leave you should want to
kind of ask around and sort of find out what
other people suppose it was all about and
what the occasion was and why you
were invited--especially when you
weren't even *you* before the invitation
came--and the you that was not yet you
accepted; and it's not surprising that
you should want to know something about
what all those legendary early party goers,
the ones who came to the party long
before you arrived, the ones they still
talk about and remember with horror or
fondness...what they supposed they
were doing there, and why they were
invited and why the party was given
in the first place, and who the host and
hostess were, and who else was there
and what such a wild party was all about
from the beginning, whenever that was,
to the end, whenever that fabled eventuation
might be imagined to take place, if ever.

## Robert McGovern

### *Encore et Encore*

The mortal struggle in erotic love
is obvious, of course: couples
tease, toy, grapple, and bite
before they pounce to bump, thump,
cry and whine in dupal pain
the agony of mutual deaths
in the centric joy of loss of self.

That selfless act begets, of course,
another love with other pains
and quite another resolution.
Early on, the gentle cuddles
ape the seminal two in making three--
but we can skip all that and all
the teeny-bopping in between
(with ego-soreness all around)
and let them grow to semi-in-
dependence and come to grips
with terminal needs in phileo love.

One hopes that manners will prevail,
but necessity of growing selves
imposes cries and whines and thumps,
mores scuffled in agony
of assertive solo flights of spite,
whose dissolutions in tears prove weak,
and back we come again at it.

No, age must make its mark:
no little death can stay that love,
for it grows in wisdom and fear--with hope
in the centric joy that grips us all.

## A Poor Player Seeks Byzantium

(Composition with Red, Yellow, and Blue,
*Piet Mondrian, 1927--my birthdate*)

Before he framed you,
only the central square
(off white and edged in black)
contained your shape:
red, blue, yellow, three other whites
escaped to infinity, or the total world
that he finally edged his own.

Your shape and I have squared a time--
so little now, it seems,
and you, of course,
are part of what we know....

But I forget ourselves:
you are there,
and he was gone in '44.

So how do I relate?
My conscious frame
can keep alive a self-hope color
until unconsciousness drop the edges
and shades escape.
And could I climb your wall,
where in the world would I fit?

Could that frame contain us both,
or would those red initials
escape with the ineffable blue?

## Scarecrow Love

We're not those young in one another's arms.
Once, though, we quivered in that state
with throbbing, open vessels and wild surmise
to that mindless grapple that deifies
homing tingle from glans to testes, mat-
ing blazing, blasting bodies to domestic arts.

The children scattered now, we tangle not
with dignity as might befit our times,
nor with arteries quite as clear. But form
presides as our ordered touch and taste warms
from knowing where and how our bodies rhyme,
whom to balance, when to smile, what to prop.

The why at this late date is obvious--
pure abstraction: tangible, tingling us.

## Personal Pollution

*(For Susan Huff)*

After the open heart,
it seems a bit pedestrian
a few weeks later
to poem the plastic
artery planted
from groin to knee
to halt my gimp.

But I came to see
a personal reprieve
in nature's end:

a nonbiodegradable
immortality.

Besides the vision
of a blob of plastic white
amid the ashes,
what do I tell
my environmental
friends?

## For Barbara at Fifty

But a little late in actual time,
from last October's ripened rite
the numbers jibe at twenty-five
to mark your staying power:
half your life, bed and board
have had and held with me,
your fractious fraction.

Good girl!

You've suffered sprains, of course,
when you may have yanged
when you should have yinned
(or turn that around),
but nothing's really been broken.
The chemistry that closed
the you
the me
fractionated, crystallized
to a curious mathematics:
one plus one equals one
more squared makes four plus
one divided by two is six
times four is twenty-four

plus the yin-yang one
has given me more
than half your life.

Well, thanks.

And though it's a little scary,
we ripen another year next month,
when over half your life is mine,
and your only hope, as I divine,
is a fractional distillation
when Malthus factors in.

## Interludes

How suddenly my world matures:
a straggling forsythia I allowed
some twenty years of sullen growth
tendered this spring fingering signs
of yellowed hope beyond itself
and now with the gravid firebushes
dims my view, stretches my neck
to safely sneak my way to the road.
Untrimmed plantings by the house,
hazelnuts that shade the grapes,
and brambles that have always skimped
now promising a jellyful of winter
shorten by a quarter hour
my weekly circlings of the yard--
all as if a Lancelot Brown
were to return to what he thought
so capable some growing ages ago.

Wipe your hand across your brow
and laugh: the worlds revolve like mowers
gathering mulch for future growth.

## Neill Megaw

### Last Words of Methuselah

*(The genealogies in Genesis have Methuselah dying in the year of the Flood, when his son Lamech had been dead five years and his grandson Noah was 600.)*

At my age, nine hundred and sixty-nine,
One gets prophetic--a kind of compensation,
Too painful remembering back, one looks ahead.
Something is going on, is shifting. The signs
Are not good. The campfires going dead,
Cattle uneasy, birds all wrong in the sky,
The well-water fouled with flies and stinking.
Noah bitten by some revelation--
The ocean rising from its ancient bed
To drown us--some such stuff, the boy's gone mad,
All day the sawing, sawing, hammering, clinking,
The thunk of the timbers: a ship to sail the sand?
As much sense as pyramids under the sea.
Well, what does it matter, my mind is going bad,
Like Noah. And Lamech dead. I see that I
Will never make that dreamt-of thousandth year.
Indeed. I see my time is come, is here.
So be it.... No, confess! It stabs like a knife:
One thousand years--now, there would have been a life!
And then, with a work like that so nearly completed,
To find, so late in the game, that I've been cheated!
Lord God, thou ownest all eternity!
Why couldn't you spare a few more years for me?
A trifle of thirty-one would have seen me through!
--And just beginning to learn a thing or two!

## Peter Meinke

### Love Poem 1990

When I was young and shiny as an apple in the good
    Lord's garden
I loved a woman whose beauty like the moon moved all the
    humming heavens to music
till the stars with their tiny teeth burst into song
and I fell on the ground before her while the sky hardened
and she laughed and turned me down softly, I was
    so young.

When I was a man sharp as a polished axe in the
    polleny orchard
I loved a woman whose perfume swayed in the air,
    turning the modest flowers scarlet and loose
till the jonquils opened their throats and cackled out loud
when I broke my hand on her door and cried I was tortured
and she laughed and refused me, only one man in a crowd.

When I grew old, owning more than my share of
    the garden,
I loved a woman young and fresh as a larkspur trembling in
    the morning's translucent coolness,
her eyes had seen nothing but good, and as the sun's gold
rolled off her wrists with reluctance, she pardoned
my foolishness, laughed and turned me down gently, I
    was so old.

And when I fell ill, rooted in a damp house spotted
    with curses,
I loved a woman whose bones rustled like insect wings
    through the echoing darkening rooms
and the ceiling dropped like a gardener's hoe toward my bed
so I stretched out my hand to her begging my god
    for mercy
and she laughed and embraced me sweetly, I was so dead.

Richard Moore

## The Cinder

Employers need outwitting;
and so, instead of quitting--
costing them, understand,
forty or fifty grand,

I managed to get *fired.*
I call myself "retired,"
but, friends, I am a *fiery*
and passionate retiree.

Leaving the hurly-burly
of life and labor early,
crazier by the minute,
I gaze at those still in it

and feel a warm sensation:
my final conflagration.
Now busily and gaily
I ignite in verse daily

and flame out in my toil
like shining from shook foil
(who cares if I sound odd
and echo Hopkins' God?)

then shrivel to a cinder
among my *toten Kinder*.
Belinda, good and just,
watches me in disgust,

light-shedding brightly orbed,
and says I'm "self-absorbed."

Unperked, unpaid--yea, pelfless--
I think I'm downright *selfless,*

dancing about and glowing
while the north wind is blowing.
Soon, mixing with that weather,
I'll vanish altogether.

## The Old Men

O Lord, teach us, us mad old men, to pray.
Eyes blinking in the sun's deceiving glow,
we are disgruntled with the light of day.

We sit unseeing where the children play.
We stand unfeeling when the breezes blow.
O Lord, teach us, us mad old men, to pray

that we may hear, as always, far away
singing of birds, sounds that we used to know...
We are disgruntled with the light of day

and angry with the objects that betray
impatient fingers, grasping, stiff and slow.
O Lord, teach us, us mad old men, to pray

gently, to taste our dinner and be gay,
delighting in the touch of things although
we are disgruntled with the light of day.

Slowly all colors, as our hairs, go gray.
Is this the only world, decaying so?
O Lord, teach us, us mad old men, to pray.
We are disgruntled with the light of day.

## In Memory of Rita Hayworth

As the Hollywood sex queen almighty
pictured in *LIFE* in your black lace nightie,
you made us slaver, snigger, chortle.
Of course, we knew that you were mortal--
    but Alzheimer's disease!
            Jeez.

## Michael Mott

### Homage to Constantine Cavafy

*"He began to see the hollowness of a life devoted to sensuality, its fragmentation and its waste."*

Poets in a Landscape: Propertius

How would you feel, old master, about that one sentence
in Professor Highet's otherwise excellent book
I wonder? I do not share your predilection
for males. I understand how such things
could be. But I do not share it. However
your celebration of particular rooms in the past,
    your ironic defiance,
your feeling that lovemaking is the one thing
to get excited about--*Agitato ma non troppo*--forever,
*that* I share. Is it true for you, me, Propertius,
that we'll never outgrow what the skin hints is real?...
Or be tricked after all by the schoolbooks and rulebooks,
our mind's taken over by rote to be rid of good sense
after bidding indecent goodbye to the senses?...
When we're old, cold, neglected grow shrill
in our skins? That I doubt. There is Yeats to disprove it,
if we want another opinion. I prefer yours. It's quieter,
more confident, too. And your smile, old Attic admirer,
when they break me in flesh may suffice to remind me
there are memories yet as we grudge the last pass
    at Thermopylae.

Lisel Mueller

## Midwinter Notes

On my shelf of photographs
the dead have come to outnumber the living.
They stand like artificial flowers
among the real ones, so lifelike
even God might be fooled.

*

My husband says spring will be early.
He says this every year,
and every year I disagree.
He needs me, the dark side
of the planetary equation.
Together we make the equinox.

*

As the world grows darker
before my eyes, the sun
sends me sharper, harder
glances off glass, off ice--
like the white light reported
by the temporarily dead,
the brightness they are teased with
and turned away from.

*

Another chance to wake up together,
accepting the invitation
of one more morning. Another chance
to push the black dream of waking alone
over the edge of the world,
where there is no life to sustain me.

*

Only after
our garden became a graveyard
strewn with shriveled leaves
did the white stem rise
from the hermetic bulb,
displaying five lavender petals:
*Colchicum autumnale*--
a brilliant contradiction,
out of phase, like an angel
strayed into Time, our world.

*

Though I fly, like the crow,
the shortest distance to death,
some knowledge will always remain foreclosed.

*

At twilight, water in roadside ditches
pulls down the last light
to be transformed from lead
into softly gleaming silver.
It has taken me years to discover
this slant conjunction of sky and water
late in the day, when the dead
are allowed their brief shining.

## What Is Left to Say

The self steps out of the circle;
it stops wanting to be
the farmer, the wife and the child.

It stops trying to please
by learning everyone's dialect;
it finds it can live, after all,
in a world of strangers.

It sends itself fewer flowers;
it stops preserving its tears in amber.

How splendidly arrogant it was
when it believed the gold-filled tomb
of language awaited its raids!
Now it frequents the junkyards,
knowing all words are secondhand.

It has not chosen its poverty,
this new frugality.
It did not want to fall out of love
with itself. Young,
it celebrated itself
and richly sang itself,
seeing only itself
in the mirror of the world.

It cannot return. It assumes
its place in a universe of stars
that do not see it. Even the dead
no longer need it to be at peace.
Its function is to applaud.

## Fugitive

My life is running away with me;
the two of us are in cahoots.
I hold still while it paints
dark circles under my eyes,
streaks my hair gray, stuffs pillows
under my dress. In each new room
the mirror reassures me
I'll not be recognized.
I'm learning to travel light,
like the juice in the power line.
My baggage, swallowed by memory,
weighs almost nothing. No one suspects
its value. When they knock on my door,
badges flashing, I open up:
I don't match their description.
Wrong room, they say, and apologize.
My life in the corner winks
and wipes off my fingerprints.

## Leonard Nathan

### Truth

*for Jamie Nathan, my grandson*

As children in the schoolroom game
whisper from one end of the class to the other
and garble the message they pass on or change it
beyond recognition, so we
pass on the truth of our kind.

My father heard it from his, something
vaguely involving God, and his father
heard it from his, and so on back
to Abraham, and so my father
passed it on to me, but God had dropped out.

And so my son heard it, a wisdom
found inside a Chinese fortune cookie:
"Be good and hope," which he will pass on
to his son, but maybe with good
missing or hope, maybe with love added.

Though love was never meant to mean so much.

### A Stroll Through the Park

Old men playing chess or checkers here
also play with time, slow to move
as if they had forever to decide
what choice will make them winners in the end.

One of them sings in a sweet, papery tenor
snatches of old love songs. One traveled
to China--why, he can't remember. One
stayed home but is no less the strange for that.

And one swears he was a cowboy. No one
believes him. He doesn't even believe himself,
although this mustang still rears up in dreams,
and always throws him, so he wakes to pain,

but feels his heart galloping away.

## Vision in the Ice Cream Parlor

When the black high school girl,
suddenly turning from her companions,
said to the elderly white man (there
to fetch chocolate milk shakes
for him and his bed-ridden wife),
"You have beautiful eyes," he blushed.

Sweet is pure disinterest, sweeter
even than the sweetness of syrup
spun in cream, almost as sweet
as love spun in young bodies.

## Retirement Home Canticle

This is in memory
of her already forgotten,
who has long since died
but patiently lives on
for these posthumous duties--
to choose between the violet
and the beige dress,

to nod back at you
if you nod at her,
to remember the shady lanes
of love that got her here
much to her amazement,
to walk the glass-eyed beagle
every last evening
of eternity
where the names of things peel
off them like old paint.

## Left-overs

Winter for the old
is like opening
the refrigerator sometime
between midnight and dawn:
in the pale arctic air
a little white village
of plastic containers snug
as igloos but greasy to touch.
Only the orange glowing
on the bottom shelf,
like a new-risen sun,
looks good enough to eat
if you were just hungry
as you stand there trying
to remember why
you stand there.

## The Old Poet

The old poet, getting smaller
each year, more Japanese--
happy enough with one pine
and the mossy rock in its shade.

His typist, older still,
makes three more mistakes
each poem, but he's too shy
to correct or let her go.

The only issues left--
the beginning and the end. Between,
pleasure marks its times
in red (or was that pain?).

He opens his eyes: O light,
but no, he's still dreaming.
He opens his eyes again.
No. Maybe the next time.

It hardly matters. Soon
he'll be so small he can slip quietly
into the painting he loves, the one
called "Snow and Spring on the Mountain."

Linda Pastan

## Narcissus at 60

If love hadn't made him clumsy,
if he hadn't fallen forward,
had never drowned
in his own perfection,

what would he have thought
about his aging face
as it altered, year after year
season by season?

In the old conspiracy
between the eye
and its reflection, love casts
a primal shadow.

Perhaps he would blame
the wrinkling surface of the pool
for what he saw
or think the blemishes

on his once smooth cheek
were simply small fish
just beneath the lethal skin
of the water.

## May 27

You can almost hold it
in your hand:
one lifetime, polished
and ready to put away,
like one of those silver watches
they give you on the last day
of work, snug
in its shammy pocket
where it won't tarnish,
won't even tick.
We fill the hours' emptied
shelves with stories
of what our children are doing,
as if they were the heroes
instead of the minor characters
they used to be, needing
to be bathed and put to bed
before the real evening
could begin. If we are simply
marking time, let us do it
prodigally, strewing the minutes
like stolen flowers
in front of us, dying
as if by accident.

## Sometimes

from the periphery
of the family
where I sit watching
my children and
my children's children
in all their bright
cacophony,

I seem to leave
my body--
plump effigy
of a woman, upright
on a chair--
and as I float
willingly away

toward the chill
silence of my own future,
their voices break
into the syllables
of strangers, to whom
with this real hand
I wave goodbye.

## Hardwood

Do these gnarled and twisted trees
feel greenness surge
at their roots the way saplings do?
When a new leaf breaks through
are they astonished,
as Sarah must have been,
at such an improbable birth?

The woodpecker, with its
firing squad rat-tat-tat, knows
each vulnerable spot on the wrinkled bark.
In a month these trees will resurrect
a shade to sit beneath.
There are stumps
to rest on everywhere.

Robert Phillips

## Survivor's Song

All my good friends have gone away.
The boisterous flight of stairs is bare.
There's nothing more I want to say.

First was Jean--she thought she was gay--
drunk nightly on *vin ordinaire.*
All my good friends have gone away.

And where is Scotty B. today?
So Southern, so doomed, so savoir-faire?
(There's nothing more I want to say.)

Sweet Hermione was third to stray.
How her monologues smoked the air!
All my good friends have gone away.

Daniel, our beer-budget gourmet,
no longer plays the millionaire.
There's nothing more I want to say

Except: My world's papier-mâché.
I need them all--weren't they aware?
All my good friends have gone away.
There's nothing more I want to say.

## The Land: A Love Letter

*for Judith*

This hill and the old house on it
are all we have. Two acres,
more or less--half crabby lawn,
half field we mow but twice a year.

Some trees we planted, most gifts
of the land. The pine by the kitchen?
Grown twice as fast as our son. The bald
elm lost the race with my hairline.

The mulberry--so lively with squirrels,
chipmunk chases, and birds--
fell like a tower in the hurricane.
My chain saw ate fruitwood for weeks.

And the juniper, the one that all but
obliterated the view? Men cut it
down to make way for the new well and water-
pump. That pump should pump pure

gold: we lay awake engineering
ways to get it paid for. But we'll never
leave this mortgaged hill: This land
is changing as we change, its face

erodes like ours--weather marks,
stretch marks, traumas of all sorts.
Last night a limb broke in the storm.
We still see it sketch the sky.

We've become where we have been.
This land is all we have, but this love
letter is no more ours than anyone's
who ever married the land.

## Kenneth Pitchford

### For Those Who Follow

Negotiating the trail gets treacherous from here on,
with fewer clues about what footholds are safest.
Keep one foot firmly rooted while raising the other.

The boldest sunflecks fall here,
dahlia sunsets, streaked iris dawns.

But however wild or unvisited it looks,
you can be sure that someone has gone before you,
a climber who lingers on only in these shadows.

A carved wood bowl, grain wrapped
around its hollow like a birdnest.

Like you, that climber pushed on after all hope failed
--to a plateau some distance farther up this slope.
When you reach *that* spot, you can celebrate indeed.

Cliffs overlooking the bald sea,
sandals untied, cast off in moonlight.

If you have any spare energy then, any more
years, resources, ideas, loves, promises,
you deserve them at last. They belong to you.

A body lying beside yours, lips open,
hands possessing you like quicksand.

But if you collapse in gauzy exhaustion here,
don't blame yourself. This terrain is truly desolate.
Few get much farther than I. At least you tried.

And sleep sweeps over you soon like
lightning, bone-stalk white forever.

David Ray

## Age

Horrid confession: yes, we were around
before t.v.,

recall bending our heads to the radio,
F.D.R.'s speeches, even the King

of England throwing in the towel
for the woman he loved.

It hurt just as much then--
Love. Made men and women

do all sorts of fool things.
Walls of Troy were already

down, of course, Abelard
and Heloise long gone,

his balls cut off, she
locked in a nunnery, hard

service after passionate love.
As for Ted Williams,

he was a baseball player,
whom some compared with Apollo,

who was a god.

## The Tomb

*"Only the nails grow"*
*Tamura Ryuichi*

A Japanese tycoon wants to take to his grave
a Van Gogh and a Picasso. He after all
owns them. But why not a Mary Cassatt,
Is he sexist? Why not an Edward Hopper
or a John Marin, is he snubbing the States?

Perhaps he could be persuaded to enlarge
his tomb just a bit--something in the style
of Forest Lawn, where the movie stars lie.
He could have a gallery leading into
the tomb--open to the public,
where they could view all his possessions,
not just the two paintings. Schoolkids
could be led through in groups--
quite educational--and the *pièce de resistance*
could be the tycoon himself.

I can see him now, kind of an almond-
eyed Jay Gatsby of a Japanese gentleman--
reclining on a red velvet chaise lounge,
whatever he likes to smoke perpetually
renewed so it burns in his stiff fingers
that nevertheless look quite natural
due to the manicurist who comes in
weekly. The children could stand
and watch him through glass. He'd have
glass eyes, of course, or amber,
which would glow with much the same intensity
as when the man still alive gazed adoringly
at his Van Gogh, his Picasso.

I myself would like to go to see
such a tomb--good for tourism, for world
trade, for keeping art relevant.
For this Japanese gentleman I'd save
for my Supersaver or sign up for a tour group,
though I plan no grand tomb of my own,
        and must look for vicarious fulfillment.

If I look around, though, I see quite a few
things I should take--treasures that mean
much to me. Not a Van Gogh this morning,
but a rumpled glad-bag that held my carrots,
a child's plastic red scissors, just right
for following the dotted line, a hat
bought in Glickman's years ago and still
serving quite well. And this poem,
of course, a gift from the muse I feared
had forgotten me--alive and well
in my hut with patched screens, flyswatter, fly.

## Knute Skinner

### A Special Occasion

Hilda is looking down on me now
where they've brought me for lunch at Johnson's,
where we used to bring them
on special occasions.
The roast beef is still tasty
if I take it in small enough bites.

Our sons and daughters are here, with their wives
and husbands.
That's Lionel and Marjorie and Elmer and Jeannie.
And that's Harriet and William and Eleanor and George.
They all look chipper enough,
though Elmer has aged since they let him go
at the bank in Hannibal.

I've shown them the letter that came
from my great grandson Ben.
He's off in the Persian Gulf.
He's defending our freedom--so William tells me.
I'm a little bit out of touch.

Hilda is up there smiling
her bittersweet smile at this fresh young kid
she met at the St. Louis World's Fair.
We used to say we would see
one hundred together.

But my brother Roscoe is here--
there in that goddammed wheelchair.
I'm glad to see Roscoe again,
even if he won't let on
that he knows who I am.
It's a good few years since he and I hauled gravel.

The others are all back at the house,
my children's children and some of their children
and some of their children's children.
So many I won't know who's missing
unless someone tells me.
They'll make me tired with their cards and boxes,
and they'll make me blind with their popping cameras.

My gift to them will simply be
that I'm still alive,
and I'll say, as I always do,
that there's nothing like it.

W.D. Snodgrass

## An Envoi, Post-turp

*(After Trans-Urethral Resectioning of the Prostate, men experience retrograde ejaculation, the semen being passed later during urination.)*

Farewell, children of my right hand and bliss.
You'll come no more but in bright streams of piss,
Never more turn my bedroom towels stiff,
Whitewash the walls or glisten on the quiff;
Never more swim like salmon or rough Norse
Invaders swarming upstream to the source.
Once, ovaries were ovaries; sperms, sperms.
In nine short months you brought us all to terms
When captive loins were sentenced by your court
To long years, lawyers' fees and child support.
You cared for just one thing--aye, that's the rub:
Each of you, at your Health and Country Club
Timed training laps, did pushups by the pool
Shunning each voice that cried, "Back, back you fools,
We'll all be killed--it's a blow job!" You hurled
Yourselves, bluff hardy semen, on the world
Like Noah's load that crested with the Flood
To populate the land and stand at stud.
Ink of my pen, you words spent ἐν ἀρχῇ,
This writer, knowing all he's cast away,
Knowing your creamy genes and DNA
Encodes our texts, pirates and then reprints us, says,
"Good night, bad cess to you, sweet prince and princesses."

## Anniversary Verses for My Oldest Wife

I vowed and vowed again
I'd marry me no more;
I hadn't met you then.
I reswear all I swore.

Too young to have known better,
You laid down, side by side,
Our differences together:
Your hasbeen; my child bride.

Through ten years you've endured
Me older than all others;
Since aging hasn't cured
Your tastes, stay thou my druthers.

Only our second night
We ended up at last;
This new dog's learned the right
Old lady'll fix you fast.

## Gary Snyder

### So Old--

Oregon Creek reaches far back into the hills.
Burned over twice, the pines are returning again.
Old roads twist deep into canyons,
    hours from one ridge to the next
The new road goes straight on the side of the mountain,
    high, and with curves ironed out.
A single hawk flies leisurely up,
    disturbed by our truck
Down the middle fork-south fork opening,
    fog silver gleams in the valley.
Camptonville houses are old and small,
    a sunny perch on a ridge,
Was it gold or logs brought people to this spot?
    a teenage mother with her baby stands by a pickup.
A stuffed life-size doll of a Santa Claus
    climbs over a porch-rail.
Our old truck too, slow down the street,
    out of the past--
It's all so old--the hawk, the houses, the trucks,
    the view of the fog--
Midwinter late sun flashes through hilltops and trees
    a good day, we know one more part of our watershed,
And have seen a gorge with a hairpin bend
    and followed one more dirt road to its end.
Chilling, so put on jackets
    and take the paved road out
Back to our own dirt road, iron stove,
    and the chickens to close in the dusk.
And the nightly stroll of raccoons.

## Breasts

That which makes milk can't
        help but concentrate
Out of the food of the world,
Right up to the point
        where we suck it,
Poison, too

But the breast is a filter--
The poison stays there, in the flesh.
Heavy metals in traces
        deadly molecules hooked up in strings
        that men dreamed of;
Never found in the world til today.
        (in your bosom
        petrochemical complex
        astray)

So we celebrate breasts
We all love to kiss them
        --they're like philosophers!
Who hold back the bitter in mind
To let the more tasty
Wisdom slip through
        for the little ones.
        who can't take the poison so young.

The work that comes later
After child-raising
For the real self to be,

Is to then burn the poison away.
Flat breasts, tired bodies,
That will snap like old leather,
        tough enough
        for a few more good days,

And the glittering eyes,
Old mother,
Old father,
        are gay.

## After T'ao Ch'ien

"Swiftly the years, beyond recall:
Solemn the stillness of this Spring morning."
I'll put on my boots & old levis
& hike across Tamalpais.
Along the coast the fog hovers,
Hovers an hour, then scatters.
There comes a wind, blowing from the sea,
That brushes the hills of spring grass.

*marin-an*

## Gerald Stern

### Bob Summers' Body

I never told this--I saw Bob Summers' body
one last time when they dropped him down the chute
at the crematorium. He turned over twice
and seemed to hang with one hand to the railing
as if he had to sit up once and scream
before he reached the flames. I was half terrified
and half ashamed to see him collapse like that
just two minutes after we had sung for him
and said our pieces. It was impossible
for me to see him starting another destiny
piled up like that, or see him in that furnace
as one who was being consoled or purified.
If only we had wrapped him in his sheet
so he could be prepared; there is such horror
standing before Persephone with a suit on,
the name of the manufacturer in the lining,
the pants too short, or too long. How hard it was
for poor Bob Summers in this life, how he struggled
to be another person. I hope his voice,
which he lost through a stroke in 1971,
was given back to him, wherever he strayed,
the smell of smoke still on him, the fire lighting up
his wonderful eyes again, his hands explaining,
anyone, god or man, moved by his logic,
spirits in particular, saved by the fire and clasping
their hands around their knees, some still worm-bound,
their noses eaten away, their mouths only dust,
nodding and smiling in the plush darkness.

## Odd Mercy

I kick a piece of leather; except the claw
it's mostly sky. Let the silkweed bury it
and let the silkweed bury the silkweed. There isn't
a particle of life there, that's if leather
can have a life. Silkweed sends its seed
to cover the body--there is grease; there are
feathers on the claw. Juice, I think,
juice of the cat, juice of the silkweed. The pods
are empty, there is no cream, only a little
white left over, dry and fluffy. Let the
nail bury the nail, let the helmet
of someone named Knute bury the helmet of someone
named Si or Cyrus. Inside the bliss is gone,
the mind is empty; it has moved from one form
of grasping to another. I lift it up,
it is a kind of football, something between
a dry tongue and a ball. I execute
a perfect drop kick, claw after claw--there still
are drop kicks in Pennsylvania. It could be
the self growing more aloof that gives me courage,
something I can hide behind. I still
freeze when I see a corpse, the spiteful dead
imitating the living, still lying there
with a hand between their thighs, or a paw lifted up
against the light. Let the clogged-up neck
bury the clogged-up neck, let the wristbone
bury the wristbone. If there is someone named Si
let there be someone named Cyrus, let him run
like Knute ran. In my thirteenth and fourteenth year
I spent my afternoons at Schenley Oval
running until it got dark. I was alone
on the ancient track.--Was it a mile and a quarter?--
I know the empty stands were still intact
the way they were when horses rounded the bend.
The palings were even intact. Let the dark boy

with the long face come and stand at the railing, let him
comb his hair, the part on the left, let him
wipe away the sweat, then look at the moon
while he waits for his father; he will spend his lifetime
waiting. If there is a brown seed on his shoulder,
if it came from the brown plant beside the fence, it is almost
lighter than life and came by air to land
as the current decided. He reaches for a twig
and breaks it off, the pods are perfect, they are
like round canoes with graceful prows and ribbing
that holds the silk together. He had vertigo--
from running, he thought--sometimes he stopped on
    a sidewalk
or under a tree to feel it--it was pleasure
he kept to himself. I still have that pleasure. Who is
the football, he or I? Who is the cat?
Am I or he? The "son of man," what is that
in the other writing? He has neither a Sears
nor a Posturepedic. Let me be the father
and bury myself. Follow me. We are
sitting on wooden boxes. We are singing
without lungs! Let the sea-horse bury
the sea-horse, let him die standing up. The foxes
have condominiums, the birds have silkweed
but my poor son doesn't have a sofa, he
and I are snoring, don't tell a soul. I can't
at my age start a second life, where will I
find another wife--at the airport?--How can I
stand in line for another job, how can I fight
for air again, what if I had to buy
new furniture? There is a cat inside. I love him
for dying. There is a way of kicking a suitcase
in front of the agents, one foot back and onto
the scale, there are tags all over, there are
books inside and underwear, the cat
is in a rage, there is silkweed, it drifts
like insulation over the brushes, it falls

like snow in the farthest pockets, there is toothpaste
and neutrogena and solex; there is a clock
I bought in Siena, it is a German clock,
a *Peter*, with three stars and a kind of forties'
face; it ticks like an ancient bomb, the size
is perfect, the paint is a little chipped, it is
a second heart for the cat and after a day
of odd mercy another one for me.

William Sylvester

## Cockles by the Sea

Sunlight splotches
high slow swells
darker than Navy blue
How vast the smell of kelp!
Our eyes clicked
She jogging in light blue Nikes
grinned
Complicity? Kindness?
Had she glanced at my thick wool cap
her hair wild?
My London Fog Navy blue coat?
CVS 5 by 2 and 1/2 inch memo book?
My noting whatever might be
between the sea
beyond the boardwalk
the aquarium at my back?
not far from Cannery Row
Sea of Cortez
Steinbeck's moon tide dream
making male dinosaurs
spurt, splatter through ginko leaves

Maybe she and I made love
ages ago and I forgot but
she'd remember
how considerate I must have been
the next day my arm around her waist
guiding her to the bathroom
"Look, look!" I said "Don't
look at me.
Look at the 19 year old boy in the mirror."

## Listening to Maggi Meyer Listening to Poetry

Your plosive "HAH!" put between de-
rision
and approval, the best ambi-
guity
for any poetry reading; your
"HAH!"
cherishing the very ironies we
love
and try to flee...when you and I were
even
younger Maggi, in the days of
strap-
less gowns, gardenias, Glenn Miller, I wore
acne
boils pointed at the back of my collar, your
"HAH!"
and mine--who would have said it first and
why?

## A Student Wrote
## Reeks of Joy
## Can You Believe It
## Reeks of Joy
## What Do They Learn in High School These Days?

outside the Legion of Honor
San Francisco
a thermal wave in the air
moves me, my youth wasted
hearing those chattering
lipsticked puffy pink faced
overstuffed dolls in my dreams

just before World War II
(Betty Friedan
where were you when I needed you most)
here, before me
a forty year old woman
jogging herself breathless
(no anorectic ballerina
tip toe with her pretty little
tutu sticking straight out)
her magnificent thigh muscles
moving sculpture through her wet leotards
her nude face wets one wisp of hair
sweat glows in her armpits
crotch
reeking with
joy

## Leonard Trawick

# On That Day

*The child is father of the man.*

When the last trumpet summons all creatures
to repossess their atoms, and we rise,
the walking archives of ourselves, in layers,
wrinkled, pillaged, marked by our terminal ills;
when skittering trilobites, glum mastodons,
drowned kittens find the place prepared for them,
and even Important People check their stubs:
then, before all dissolves, I'd like to quiz
my younger selves, sent home this final time--
why did they leave such scrappy records, and why
couldn't they all have just stayed on? In turn,
no doubt, they'll ask me, elder heir, to expound
sage views on life, love, fame, and fortune. And--
why'd I let the old place get so run down?

Lewis Turco

## Gerascophobia: The Fear of Aging

Somewhere within these houses a woman looks
into a mirror and wonders why, or who
or when today has turned to mist and the sky
to leaves. Wherever else one looks a squirrel
seems to have a small request, but it

will still be weeks before the oaks manage
the feat of acorns. For now, the sun has gone
to earth, the trees brood in a pall of breathless
forenoon along the early summer streets,
among the late-arising neighbors. Here and there

a car coughs and begins to idle. The morning
papers materialize upon the verandas.
A schoolbus turns the corner saffron and then
disappears in a puff of smoke and gas.
In her room a woman wears a sapphire.

She looks into a mirror. Perhaps she lacks
that certain blue capacity, if she's lucky.
And if she's not, well, still she has the day,
the mist, the oaks, the squirrels, the mooning night
and the long dream of what is forever lost.

## A Song of Time's Passage

A world of cold water's flowed over the dam,
And the dam looks mossy, damn mossy, my friend.
Chill winters have weathered her, and warm springs
Have leaked through the sluice where the bullfrog sings
The peeper's green song that never shall end
Down by the dam, friend. Dam your eyes--
Never say "was," say "will be" and "am."
That person's a fool who blubbers and sighs.

The millwheel races to beat the clock;
The chime strikes out--it takes its toll
As time consumes the current hour
Like a pickerel striking to devour
The minnows of minutes, to take them whole
Down by the dam, friend. Dam your eyes--
Don't fish on a sandbank; cast from a rock!
No mossback takes good anglers by surprise.

Our summers have bobbed on the crests of our falls;
The millrace runs, the pond grows shallow.
Reeds bristle like beards where beavers go deep,
Where old newts burrow and turtles sleep.
The willow withers, the lilly, the mallow
Down by the dam, friend; dam your eyes--
It's only a puddle. If ageing palls,
Go spout in the ocean--that never dries.

## Chronophobia: The Fear of Time

He hears his timepiece ticking in the night
beside his bed. Down the shadowed hall
each ponderous hour is rung by the standing clock.
He jerks awake and wonders why he has
these instruments of torment in his home.

He lies awake and hears the sandgrains fall
between the walls. The deathwatch beetle marks
behind his bed the moments of his life--
will daylight never dawn? Is all the world
forever lost in labyrinthine gloom?

He comes awake, rises and leaves his room
to wander down the hall. He hears the hour
rung by the standing clock. Its pendulum
swings through the moon, describing a silver arc
sixty times a minute--he hears the chatter

as though the sounds were rising from his brain.
Is all the world forever lost in sand
falling between the walls, deserts composed
of the moments of his life? He returns to bed
and hears his timepiece ticking in the night

## About the Young

The world is all about the young;
    we elders are wrung out of it
though we continue here among
the relevant. The clock has rung
    one chime too often. Our phlegm and spit

are all the juices we have left--
    what would we do with more than these?
Our bedward turns are less than deft
these nights, our winding sheets bereft
    of art. There are no mysteries.

Then what's the point? The future's all,
    and when there's none, or very little,
we hang our portraits on the wall
and walk away from hall to hall
    to find a place to sit and whittle

away our last few hacking days
    and piddle away our aching nights.
The world is all about the ways
The young make young and not the grays
    that color our brows with northern lights.

But looking back at all the mess,
    the scrabble, the lyrics badly sung
to music composed in wild distress,
one shakes one's head and mutters, "Yes,
    the world *is* all about the young."

## Alberta Turner

### Thread

The dead are away from home   A truck drives up and men in uniform unscrew the house numbers and disconnect the phone   One brings out a quart of milk   one a pitcher of goldfish   A child unbuckles the collar of the hound chained to the porch   A neighbor cuts lilacs and leaves a note
Two passersby unhook the clothesline and count the pins
And an officer carts a freezer to the curb and takes the door off   The last one out   a woman   carries a jar of screws and a box of threads   across the street   "The Byrnes are dead" she explains   "Will you keep these for them?   No one can say when they'll be home"

### Seventeen Ways to Make Sure You Are Still Alive

Chew a grass blade.
Draw a drop of honey down a honeysuckle stamen.
Pull pine needles out of your hair.
Listen to crows.
Work without gloves.
Don't mention *cancer, cataracts, coronaries,* or *teeth*.
Fill a wastebasket. Fill another wastebasket.
Worry, sneeze, laugh.
Pull off a scab to see if you still bleed.
Tear the rotted shingles off your roof.
Notice children, how they shriek.
Worry, laugh.
Pull off the scab again.
Take the stone wall apart, scrub the stones.
Hold very small things lightly in both hands.
Pull off the scab.
Lift the child "who cries in the lane" into your arms.

## Speech

Language of laugh and leap
alphabet of fun and grin,
when I am broken from my stem,
how shall I mean?

Now sit beside Aunt Mildred's ghost
and bring her news of her son's
new wife: an eyebrow plucked
and an earlobe pricked?

When I am gone and even the word
for *word* is gone, how shall I gloat?

Even the smallest cub can growl, cuff,
play war, pretend, cuff again.
And the old bear plays his broken
claws and yellow teeth on slower
rabbits and on younger sheep.

Oh, Language, in your stocking cap
and mitts, how shall I find Jesus
or Figaro? How hail them, ask their
names? And if they don't remember,
how explain?

## Parting Branches, Lifting Grasses

Alone in the universe--that's easy,
only one self to compose, edit, read.
Water will fall without me and crash
and repair itself, ease a twig into an eddy,
raft a dragonfly across, wet me.

Animals are more difficult. Words worry them.
Had a long talk with a gray cat. She crouched
on my porch and snarled, dared, reviled.
At a distance I purred and chirped--all that nonsense
about how pretty she was, and she got the point
and explained in every inflection of miaow
how she'd been turned out, chased, deprived.
I heard. She thanked me for the milk.

Women and men are hard, like holding a fistful
of wires: every time I pull one, something
it's not attached to jerks. Or like a row of shoes:
they all fit, but I can't walk.
A metal stake shouts, "STOP."
A grown man asks, "Who are you?"

Admit it. I'm alone. The arm I take
just hangs. The hand I shake's a glove.
Frogs don't know I'm there. Even eggs
don't know I've eaten them.
A whole skyful of gods has slid back on its rod
into the wall. I go about with a bit of cheese,
making fur noises, tasting my hair.

## Man and Wife

They touched noses. She whistled Onward Christian
Soldiers. He let the cat out. He thought he didn't
need her--much. He thought her thoughtless--asking
questions, but not listening, giving answers, but
not explaining. The huge corsages at birthdays
grew more huge. At Christmas, the books on old barns
or sailing ships grew more expensive.

She had a gene for sadness. He deplored it.
Did she just need him, not love him? Those words
had been spoken. Perhaps she should have told
him at the start that the only kind of man
she could love was a man she could worship.
Once, being nervous, she accidentally called him
"father."

She never cooked a hot meal, though he
mentioned it often, but he never had to wait
to use the car or the bathroom. They worked
for hours in separate rooms, then one would stretch
and make coffee, and they'd drink it with their
elbows on the sink.

Two knobby souls--they knew exactly what living
meant together. Mostdays he thought it worth
the trouble. She did too, mostdays.

John Updike

## To a Dead Flame

Dear X, you wouldn't believe how curious
my eyebrows have become--jagged gray wands
have intermixed with the reddish-brown, and poke
up toward the sun and down into my eyes.
It hurts, a self-caress that brings tears
and blurred vision. Aches and pains! The other day
my neck was so stiff I couldn't turn my head
to parallel-park. Another man
would have trusted his mirrors, but not I;
I had the illusion something might interpose
between reality and its reflection, as happened with us.

The aging smell, X--a rank small breeze wafts upward
when I shed my underwear. My potency,
which you would smilingly complain about,
has become as furtive as an early mammal.
My hair shows white in photographs, although
the barber's clippings still hold some brown.
At times I catch myself making that loose mouth
old people make, as if one's teeth don't fit,
without being false. *You're well out of it*--
I tell you this mentally, while shaving
or putting myself to bed, but it's a lie.

The world is still wonderful. Wisps of mist
were floating off your old hill yesterday,
the hill where you lived, in sight of the course
where I played (badly) in a Senior Men's
Four-Ball in the rain, each green a mirage.
I thought of us, abed atop that hill,
and of how I would race down through your woods
to my car, and back to my life, my heart

enormous with what I newly knew--
the color of you naked, the milk of your sighs--
through leaves washed to the glisten of fresh wounds.

What desperate youthful fools we were, afraid
of not getting our share, our prize in the race,
like jostling marathoners starting out,
clumsy but pulsingly full of blood.
You dropped out, but we all drop out, it seems.
You never met my jealous present wife;
she hates this poem. The living have it hard,
not living only in the mind, but in
the receding flesh. Old men must be allowed
their private murmuring, a prayer wheel
set spinning to confuse and stay the sun.

## Elderly Sex

Life's buried treasure's buried deeper still:
a cough, a draft, a wrinkle in the bed
distract the search, as precarious as
a safecracker's trembling touch on the dial.
We are walking a slack tight wire, we
are engaged in unlikely acrobatics,
we are less frightened of the tiger than
of the possibility the cage is empty.

Nature used to do more--paroxysms
of blood and muscle, the momentous machine
set instantly in place, the dark a-swim,
and lubrication's thousand jewels poured forth
by lapfuls where, with dry precision, now
attentive irritation yields one pearl.

## Theodore Weiss

### The Last Day and the First

The stocky woman at the door,
with her young daughter "Linda" looking
down, as she pulls out several copies
of *The Watchtower* from her canvas bag,
in a heavy German accent asks me:
"Have you ever thought that these
may be the last days of the world?"

And to my nodding "Yes, I have,"
she and the delicate, blonde girl
without a further word, turning tail,
sheepishly walk away.
            And I feel
for them, as for us all, this world
in what may be its last days.
And yet this day itself is full
of unbelief, that or marvelously
convincing ignorance.
            Its young light
O so tentative, those first steps
as of a beginning dance (snowdrops
have already started up, and crocuses
we heard about last night the teller's
children quickly trampled in play)

make it hard not to believe that we are
teetering on creation's brink all over
again. And I almost thrill with fear
to think of what will soon be asked
of us, of you and me;
            am I at least
not a little old now (like the world)

to be trembling on the edge
of nakedness, a love, as Stendhal
knew it, "as people love for the first
time at nineteen and in Italy"?

Ah well, until I have to crawl
on hands and knees and then can crawl
no more, so may it every Italian-
returning season be, ever the last
day of this world about to burst
and ever for blossoming the first.

## An Old Cart

(*On being asked to write a poem*
*thirteen lines or less*
*for an English-Italian anthology*)

Thirteen lines? After seventy years
what's left to keep or say?
A few words things are struggling
to shrug off
like moldy skins.

An old cart, once crammed with hides
much coveted--its horse a jackass
after all, half-crippled--creaking
to a stop.
Maybe this way is best,
the space around me growing
and nothing to get in the way
of nothing.

## Evelyn Wexler

### End Zone

The ramps too steep to negotiate,
we are herded into a huge arena.
There are guards at all the exits.

We are gathered, the gray people,
our tongues like furred snakes,
to talk about the future.
The hope of a plastic bag,
a doctor friend promises 20-30 seconals
will do it.
Yes, but the children.

We pass around remnants
of photographs. Pallid, some of us nod,
others have forgotten the figures.
Who was that child,
the sun dazzling her eyes?
We pretend to remember.

Like echoes from a distant future
there soars a vast muttering,
the sound of leaves drowned.
The brain thins, drains.
It's the only game in town.

Ruth Whitman

## Old Love

Familiar, the face you now see
when you look at me belongs to
the young woman perched thirty-five
years ago on the arm of a
sofa, swinging her shapely leg,
wearing a skirt the color of
sunrise. The face is unlined, the
hair long, black, swept into a bun
or braided into a regal
crown. You don't see the cropped gray hair,
the thickened waist or the wrinkled
skin. And I look at you and see
the slender bridegroom pausing at
the door, searching the room, his hair
falling over his eyes, the eyes
bright, hopeful, caressing: you lift
me up and we slide into each
other, young and old, wrinkled, smooth,
like Mozart's Adagio, *con*
*amore,* tender, heartbreaking.

## Old Houses

I wear this house like a barrel
to cover my struts
and I see:
    the plaster's getting veined.
    Tender clapboards won't stand
    too much more rain.
    Inside
    the wallpaper's crepy
    where the storm came in.

Looking out from inside
it's hard to tell:
will a coat of spanking paint
make the trim seem new again?

I've seen other women preen
to the image in their eyes,
picturing moviestar lips,
a dashing lilt to the head,
    while in the mirror
    looking back
    an old mask
    props up its wrinkles
    with a kissed out mouth.

But I feel like a virgin in the dark.
I hear my voice like a child's
enter the telephone
and come out no older.

    How come this new me
    is looking out of an old house?

Harold Witt

## So Far

So far not too bad but that's illusion--
I'll feel worse after more infusion;

the more pumped in, the more I have to piss.
The nurse aid says "Please urinate in this"

and so I do, and read and watch TV.
Morning the nurse changes the IV,

blood pressure good, blood drawn from my arm,
the sun slants in, the day is starting warm.

I'm not yet weak; I'll walk the corridors
and look in those prophetic hospice doors.

## Defenseless

Defenseless, I go over to the clinic.
Mary drives me and I get infused--
neupogen again--though not a picnic
there are things about which we're amused.

"General Hospital" is on TV--
Bella says she's watched it now and then.
There's blue-eyed Julia who's a real beauty--
gorgeous--and so are some of the men.

Not much like Kaiser--and there goes the needle
into my arm. Oh I'd rather be
Jagger with that smile and widow's peak
than pale and chemo-bald, past seventy.

## Cell Mates

We swap hospital stories--what we're in for--
he says being here's like being in jail;
short, goateed and a kind of stentor,
he'll have a treadmill and it might well fail,

has had a hip replaced and needs another.
I tell him of the chemotherapy,
all the beeping and the fuss and bother,
a masked nurse enters with V p 16

and hangs the bag of poison and we joke.
Will this power work or won't it work?
I heard him moaning all night as I woke.
Parole or more of this stir? Buddy, good luck.

## Low Grade

Finally I hear from Dr. Tashima--
a low grade cancer on my prostate gland,
not too bad--or am I just a dreamer,
burying my ostrich fear in sand?

A few abnormal cells--or so he says--
slow growing--I could live to ninety-five.
It's the lymphoma that I have to face--
aggressive chemo so I'll stay alive.

Pacifist am I? Yes, but not in this.
I'm getting out my killer dogs and guns.
Goodbye, my love--though not a farewell kiss--
I'm off to finish off those errant ones.

## Biopsy

"Lie on your left side in the foetal position--
move your butt a little lower down."
At least he isn't doing an incision.
I am in a lovely hospital gown

open at the back, and Dr. Tashima,
rubber gloved, shoves a finger in--
only one? It feels like a reamer.
I'm not quite screaming but I almost am.

The nurse who's helping tells me I should breathe--
deeply, that is; then it's the ultrasound
sliding into my anus; angry bees
seem to be buzzing in a hole they've found.

All right, now the needle. It goes *click*,
just like a rattrap, and it hurts.
Doctor is your job to make me sick?
I felt OK but now I'm feeling worse.

That's it. Except the finger once again
pushing on the gland. Lie there a while.
"The room keeps dizzily turning for some men."
"Thank you, Doctor." But my lips won't smile.

## John Woods

### Playing

Once you said, could we play?
The room was hot, the blinds reddened us.
There we lay, my stringy body slow to rouse.

Carib node, swart expresso,
if you were an alligator, only your eyes
would bead above the murky water.

I took to you like the Nurser Infante,
wild for the New World
and its warm water and miracles.

We can do anything we want, you said,
and we did everything we knew.
I had promised

three hours of love.
Then, after a half hour:
"Now what do we do?"

### How She Goes

Once before, yes, more than once,
a woman took away her whipping hair,
her kitchen trebles,
into other rooms with different mirrors.

I know there is work to be done.
Children need to know the fist and palm,
the heart pains of fathers,
the ways mothers become snapshots.

I find a sprouting comb behind the bureau.
She took away the calendar
where she had marked her blood,
the fuming sauces,
the magic boots that made her tall.
Once again, a woman has taken away
her dark noisy grace.

I sit here in another April,
the house loud with silence.
Here is where my children crayoned their heights.
Here is where my gentle wife died out of her pain.
Here is where a woman
has put her gold chains in a little box
and has gone out the door.

## Tulip Tree

Tulip, tulip tree,
    when I buried your burlap roots
you were shorter than my sons.
    They have followed their shadows.
In late spring
    great waxy flowers
ignite in your dark foliage.

You live so long
    only the stars amaze you.
My father and mother,
    my wife, my lover could not
stay for me as your deep autumn
    shadow drifts into the garden.
Perhaps I'll press my face
    against your trunk, feeling
the deep roots and wind sway.

## Nancy Means Wright

### Mastectomy

Baring the left breast,
all that is precious cast
to the winds the virgins run
the Olympic track. Their toes
squash in and out of the April
ooze, their breath outwhistles
the siren's; the nipples sweat on
the swinging stalks like pink fruits.

Invisible woman, I wait at the side,
the dampness peels away my skin, I
move weightless as fog against
the finish line and beyond
the boundaries of bone;
defiance wreathes my
wet brow, I lean
into the wind.

## Grace Enters Armageddon

She sweeps across the lawn to
meet him, one-breasted woman
of sixty-seven, broad brimmed hat
riding low over an auburn wig,
Queen Anne's lace in her hefty
arms and pink and white snap
dragons. He waits by a peony
bush, gold rings in his sweaty
palm, white duck legs that won
the '39 Croquet Marathon rooted
in the grass like a wicket;
his glasses flash in the sun.

On
she goes, Vermont Venus in size
eleven sandals: her toes dazzle
pink, the sun dimples her elbows,
eyes glint green in the damp
pouches of skin. She's had it all:
hired man, two hundred acres of farm
land ripe as old pond water,
her own way in a house without
husband; if the cat howled at two
in the morning, it was Grace who
forgot to put it out.

The fiddle
drives her forward, she's almost
there: the sun irons him into
a silhouette; her mind is ablaze
like his spectacled eyes. She
ploughs into his presence (a-
mazing Grace); she's taller than
he by a thumb; the wind drums
in her ears, a cow bellows
in the corn. The mare gallops
along the fence; he'll catch her
as she comes.

David Zeiger

## For My Birthday

my daughter gives me
a personal capsule of history
from Library of Congress archives--
an original issue of the *New York Times*
published the day I was born.

Yellow with age,
edges brittle and crumbling--
metaphor for my self?--
I lift it gently from the clear
vinyl envelope enclosed
in leather folder No. 123668
to read the world I was entering:

HARDING ASSUMES REAL LEADERSHIP AS
 CONGRESS LAGS
RUSSIA ARMS FOR WAR AS MILLIONS STARVE
8 DROWNINGS MAR DAY FOR BATHERS.
On the day I am born, local thunder showers
are forecast to greet my arrival.
Three-piece Men's Suits sell at Iverson & Heneage
for forty-six dollars
and Fiorello LaGuardia gets set to run
on a five-cent fare platform plank.

Selling for two cents in Greater NY,
four cents elsewhere, pinched words
in narrow columns
speak decorously
in hushed tones.

On the day I am born
a jealous lover shoots his rival
and hangs himself.
A man angered by a trolley
smashes the car door
and two youths are arrested
for killing an 85-year-old woman.

*Special Care Instructions* warn me
to keep these pages from the light
as they are "highly subject
to deterioration from exposure
to atmospheric conditions."
At risk of flaking away the rest,
I explore no further, replacing the sheets
in their plastic shell, fragments
peeling away at every motion.
The sound of time drifts in mist.
I exist. The world burns. Over
and over it happens.